Money and the Me

MONEY
AND THE
MARKETS

An Astrological Guide

Graham Bates
and
Jane Chrzanowska Bowles

Aquarian
An Imprint of HarperCollinsPublishers

Aquarian
An Imprint of HarperCollins*Publishers*
77–85 Fulham Palace Road
Hammersmith, London W6 8JB

1160 Battery Street
San Francisco, California 94111–1213
Published by Aquarian 1994

2 4 6 8 9 7 5 3 1

A catalogue record for this book
is available from the British Library

ISBN 1 85538 370 5

Printed and bound in Great Britain by
Mackays of Chatham PLC, Chatham, Kent

Contents

Acknowledgements

We would like to thank Charles Harvey, for many useful discussions over the years, and also Mike Harding, for his help with information and research. We would also like to thank Eileen Campbell, whose original, pathfinding vision provided the inspiration that enabled this book to be written. Thanks also to Andy Black at Perfect Information, for helping us with company research for Chapter 6. We would like to thank Martin Davis and Sean Lovatt of Matrix UK for help in producing the astrological charts. Jane would like to extend her deepest, heartfelt gratitude to David and Lucie Bowles, who provided endless moral support, technical expertise, patience and understanding – not necessarily in that order! Without their help, writing this book would have been an impossible task. Finally Graham would like to thank Christeen and Mark for their friendship, support and willingness to listen over the years! Without them, this work might never have been completed.

1

An Introduction to Financial Astrology

A NEW APPROACH TO FINANCIAL CYCLES FOR THE 1990S

As the recession of the early 1990s casts its departing shadow on the horizon, there is a growing consensus in the business community that in the main, economists have failed us. In the halcyon days of the late 1980s, ministers, mandarins and market analysts alike were, to all intents and purposes, blissfully unaware that the worst recession since the Second World War was just around the corner, for their speeches, pronouncements and forecasts gave no hint of it. But as the decade turned, and the economy slid into recession, the confident, self-assured ethos of the Eighties gave way to a disturbing period of pessimism and uncertainty, and the growing sense that the old economic models were no longer working. As each fulsomely positive, but erroneous, prediction of recovery was followed in swift succession by another, it became increasingly obvious that traditional forecasting techniques were no longer effective. In fact, they had totally failed.

In the light of this manifest failure of orthodox economics, one of the most noticeable developments in business thinking has been a vigorously renewed interest in the business cycle. Whenever the economy sinks into recession, it provides a salutary reminder of how powerful a force this cycle can be, and how potent the influence it exerts on commerce, business and ordinary people. The business cycle can make fortunes, or destroy them at a stroke. Time and again, its fluctuations have overturned governments, inspired revolutions and, in the 1930s, left literally millions of people jobless and destitute. Given its power, it is easy to see why the task of predicting the precise turning-points of the economy engages so many of the finest minds in business, banking and government. Why also, in the closing years of this century, the whole question of the business cycle – or rather cycles, since there is not just a single regular cycle operating, but a number of interacting cycles – has once again become uppermost in peoples' minds.

The concept of viewing the unfolding pattern of economic activity from a cyclical perspective features prominently in the writings of contemporary economic authorities, such as William Rees-Mogg, James Dale

Davidson and William Houston,[1] who use the evidence of history to show that not only do business and finance work in cycles, but also that these cycles are non-linear. Rees-Mogg and Davidson ascribe the ineffectiveness of standard economic models to the fact that they are totally unable to explain these non-linear, irregular cycles. Despite the reluctance of mainstream economics to acknowledge the non-linearity of economic activity, a growing body of evidence has emerged to support the thesis that the economy has an underlying structure that is essentially irregular and cyclical. In the 1920s, the work of the Russian economist Kondratieff showed that there was a 'long wave' of roughly 60 years that determined the business cycle. This 'long wave' of expansion and contraction does not occur at regular intervals, however, but has a length of approximately 47 to 60 years. The Kondratieff 'long wave' provided a basis for predicting both the Great Depression of the 1930s and the recession of the 1990s, but was too ill-defined to yield the kind of precise forecasts that are necessary for detailed business planning. To quote Rees-Mogg and Davidson:

> The fact that cause and effect operate in cycles as well as in a straight line, implies that more effort should be invested in analysing the economic long wave, and the other cycles of history. This is likely to happen, as the work of notepad historians is transformed by the computer.[2]

At first sight, the work of Kondratieff and other cycles researchers such as Clement Juglar (whose nine-year cycle is also widely used in business) appears to further confound and complicate the whole process of business forecasting, rather than simplify it. For how can forecasters have any systematic way of knowing when these cycles are likely to turn? It is one thing to identify a fixed-length cycle, but quite another to predict a sequence of related, but irregular cycles. The truth remains that for forecasters who work in the conventional way, no solution to this problem can be found. But the revolution in information technology that transformed the entire financial sector in the 1980s also brought with it a means whereby businessmen and investors could at last begin to make use of the world's most comprehensive system of cycles analysis: financial astrology. For financial astrology is, in essence, the study of cycles. And for those who wish to know how the cycles that determine the financial future will unfold, it is an indispensable field of inquiry.

Astrology is the world's oldest method of cyclical analysis and its origins lie deep in the mists of antiquity. Its techniques were used in every ancient civilisation of the world to forecast the annual harvests that formed the mainstay of the early economy. Financial astrology is a specialized branch of astrology that has, in the twentieth century, finally come of age. From its pioneering days in the 1900s, it has become a highly codified empirical discipline that uses the evidence of past economic cycles and effects as the basis for predicting the financial future. J. P. Morgan, one of the richest men of his generation, employed the noted astrologer Evangeline Adams to advise him on how the prevailing planetary cycles were likely to manifest in business and finance. For, as J. P. Morgan knew, not only do the predictions of financial astrologers compare very well with more orthodox forecasts, they are also far more precise. Using astrology, we can predict exact turning-points in both the economy and the stock market many years in advance. In the case of the stock market often to the *exact day* – as we will show.

The most outstanding contribution that financial astrology has made to business and financial forecasting, however, is its ability to identify and predict irregular financial cycles. For the research of recent years has shown that the planetary cycles of astrology correlate closely – in many cases, exactly – with the irregular cycles of business and finance. Using these cyclical techniques allowed its practitioners to predict the 1990s recession as far back as 1988 – at a time when other forecasters claimed that a downturn was highly unlikely.

Financial astrology provides a vital key to understanding the emerging non-linear paradigm of economic reality, for it is the *only* forecasting system whose methodology can explain the complex, interacting and variable length financial cycles actually found in the real world. The financial astrology of the 1990s thus points the way forward for all who wish to acquire a genuine insight into the underlying forces that shape economic reality, and thereby gain a measure of control over their own financial lives.

WHO USES FINANCIAL ASTROLOGY – AND WHY

In many countries in the Orient, particularly Hong Kong and India, astrological analysis has been practised in some form or other almost continuously throughout history. Many Asian businessmen and government officials insist on consulting an astrologer before taking important decisions and, over the last decade, astrology has begun to gain a more serious audience in the West. A feature writer in *The Economist* (22 December 1984), after discussing the reliance on the stars of some Asian politicians, asked:

Is there anything in astrology? It would be impolite to dismiss outright the beliefs of many thoughtful people. Hinduism sees man and the universe as essentially in harmony, so why should the planets not affect people's lives? Elizabeth I may have been the last English monarch to have employed an astrologer. But a number of industrialists, mostly in America, have said they benefit from astrological advice, and they cannot all be loonies.

In line with this viewpoint, the use of astrology for financial forecasting in business grew steadily throughout the 1980s, especially in the United States, where businessmen are particularly noted for their pragmatic approach to new ideas. But in more conservative circles in the UK, prejudice against astrology still lingers, largely due to the mistaken belief that all astrology comes from the same stable as the 'Sun Sign' columns of the tabloids. The truth is, there are as many different schools of astrology as there are approaches to forecasting, and the kind of complex financial analysis which forms the subject-matter of this book bears about as much resemblance to the 'Sun Sign' columns of the popular newspapers as a Porsche to a pushbike! Indeed, the financial astrology of the 1990s encapsulates and embodies a cycles-based system which places it at the very forefront of current business thinking.

Financial astrology has also long been popular among the wealthier members of society. Throughout the century, it has been used by many extremely rich and influential people, including J. P. Morgan and Sheikh Yamani. This 'billionaire' factor alone would render astrology worthy of further investigation by those who are seeking to increase their own wealth in turn. But the real reason why financial astrology has begun to find greater acceptance as a forecasting tool is the formidable string of predictive successes it has produced in recent years.

In the run-up to the fourth anniversary of Black Monday, the day in October 1987 when the New York Stock Exchange experienced its worst crash for many years, Reuters News Agency asked a number of leading City analysts to assess the chances of the market taking another tumble in October 1991. Their forecasts differed widely and significantly only one of them pinpointed 15 November as *the* day when trouble could be expected on the international markets. This sole analyst was a financial astrologer – Graham Bates, the co-author of this book – and when Wall Street duly plunged by 120 points that fateful Friday, he was inundated with calls from market-watchers wanting to know exactly how he had managed to predict the exact day of the fall.

The American financial astrologer, the late Lieutenant Commander David Williams made over $1 million in the stock market between 1982 and 1987 using his astrological methods to buy into the market as it was rising and to sell at the top. Williams was for many years head of purchasing for Consolidated Edison in New York, and his track record as a forecaster in the financial markets was most impressive.

The UK financial astrologer Daniel Pallant also has an extensive client base in the financial sector. Like several of his colleagues, he foresaw the 1987 Black Monday crash well in advance and got out of the market as it peaked, helping many of his clients do the same. Following his successes, Pallant was commissioned to write a series of articles describing his techniques for the *Financial Times*.

UK astrologer Charles Harvey predicted the recession of the 1990s, along with the sharp decline in the UK housing market, and published his predictions in 1988, when mainstream economists were vehemently denying the possibility of recession. The previous year, Harvey and his colleague Mike Harding had successfully pinpointed 19 October, Black Monday, as the day when the 1987 UK bull market would end.

Finally, few forecasters could have envisioned the startling volatility of British interest rates in September 1992, when rates went up 5 per cent one day and promptly came down again the next! All was foreseen, however, by German economist and financial astrologer Dr Hans Lenz, who wrote in his summer newsletter (published that August), that September would be an interesting month for British interest rates, which were likely to both rise and fall within that four-week span.

Financial astrology's recent track record clearly shows that it has much to offer the world of business. The time has come for prejudice to be put aside in favour of a more practical, open-minded attitude. For if astrology works, as it clearly does, why not use it?

HOW DOES FINANCIAL ASTROLOGY WORK?

Readers will doubtless be saying at this point, 'Yes, that's all very well, but *how* does it work?' – and it's here that we encounter a curious paradox. Astrology works, that much is obvious. But no one has ever really discovered how. For although there is a huge body of evidence which shows that planetary cycles correlate with business and financial cycles, as well as many cycles in nature, the mechanism that links the cycles of astrology to cycles in the world still remains a mystery.

No modern astrologer believes, as his historic predecessors once did, that the rocks in the sky are directly responsible for events on earth, but rather that the relationship is one of correspondence – in other words, 'As above, so below'. The fact that this relationship does indeed exist is validated by the empirical evidence that so many generations of astrologers have amassed throughout history: the facts of the planetary positions; and the facts of what took place in the past when a particular influence occurred. For financial astrology is in no way an occult activity, but is rather a rule-based forecasting approach that rests on a bedrock of rational inquiry and hard historical evidence.

Our present position is akin to that of a medieval 'scientist' who notes that the sea seems to rise and fall during the day, thereby producing the tides. He notes the twice-daily high and low tide, and notes that they occur at different times each day. Sometimes the high tide is higher than normal, and this takes place at the New and Full Moons. Sometimes it is less high, at the Quarter Moons – but the effect is not constant. When the wind blows off the sea, the tide can be very high indeed, even at the Quarter Moons. Our poor medieval scientist had to wait until Newton's theory of gravity provided a coherent explanation for these clearly observed effects. The Sun and Moon exert a gravitational pull on the sea, and gravity causes the high and low tide – but were someone to have suggested to the medieval scientist that the tides were *caused* by the Sun and Moon, he would no doubt have dismissed it. Until Newton appeared on the scene, no explanation was possible. So astrology, in a sense, is awaiting a 'twenty-first-century Newton' – one who will finally discover the mechanism by which the planetary cycles actually bring about their effects in the world.

This book will show that there is strong evidence for an astrological effect in the financial sector and we hope our work may inspire scientists to search for an new explanation of astrology. The resulting research may well open up many fields of inquiry that have hitherto remained unexplored and hopefully lead to insights that will deepen our understanding, not just of the world of business and finance, but of all aspects of our lives.

HOW CAN FINANCIAL ASTROLOGY HELP YOU IN BUSINESS?

As the experience of the last few years has shown, the business cycle is a force to be reckoned with, and no matter how well established growth appears to be, the economy will always go into recession again at some point in the future. Knowing exactly when recessions are most likely to occur is a great boon for any business. In the late 1980s, UK astrologers saw that the Jupiter–Saturn triple cycle, one of the main determinants of recession, was about to hit a crucial point, thus making a severe economic downturn a real possibility. The nation's astrologers recorded their forecasts in the press and the accuracy of their predictions soon became only too apparent.

By using the longer-term cycles of astrology, the ebb and flow of economic growth need no longer be a source of financial uncertainty. Major economic turning-points can be pinpointed many years ahead, which facilitates investment and planning at every level. Those in business who can foresee a downturn in demand can take effective action to protect their enterprise. If they know that a forthcoming recession is likely to be tough rather than mild, expansion plans can be slowed down and borrowings reduced. Similarly, when rivals are still shrouded in gloom, but astrology has shown there is light at the end of the recessionary tunnel, they can confidently prepare for the good times ahead. Understanding the planetary cycles helps position a business to take full advantage of the upturn when it comes, and steal a march on less well-informed competitors.

In addition, investors and speculators will find it most useful to learn how stock market cycles correlate with short-term planetary cycles, for these provide a close match with market events. As we shall see, astrology allowed not only major stock market events such as 1987's Black Monday and the Wall Street Crash of 1929 to be pinpointed well ahead of time but also many other major turning-points and sudden moves in the market. The shrewd investors who already used its methods were able to sell at the top and maximize their return.

The astrological insights into the UK stock market presented in this book are highly reliable, as they are based on observations of consistent effects observed over many years. Stock market astrology is not based on conjecture or guesswork, but solid experience, and using its methods can save you a great deal of time. You can read all the latest stock broker's research, read the financial press from to cover, listen to all the conventional sources of stock market advice – and still be no better informed than anyone else. But using financial astrology gives you a great advantage, for it reveals all the hidden cyclical influences at work behind the scenes, and provides a unique perspective on what's *really* happening in the market. It can tell you when periods of unbounded optimism are coming, and when the bubble is likely to burst; when there's likely to be an atmosphere of undue pessimism (and stocks are undervalued) and when panic and uncertainty will rule the day. Correctly applied, financial astrology is a major tool in your forecasting armoury, a tool that gives you a real edge over less well-informed investors in markets which are notoriously susceptible to the instincts of the 'herd'.

Financial astrology is also useful for business and investment planning within your own company. Using your company birthchart as a
business 'road-map', you can identify the strengths and weaknesses that
exist in your enterprise, and take the right action at the right time. In
Chapter 6, we'll see how Amstrad ran into severe difficulties due to a
planetary influence that suggested a lack of structure – a shortcoming
that became all too evident in 1988/9, but which could have been spot-
ted from the outset by using astrology – how Next nearly came to grief
through expanding at the wrong time, thus going against the planetary
influences, but how Virgin Atlantic did well under the very same influences, because it focused on consolidation rather than growth. And
finally, how the notoriously newsworthy history of Polly Peck is plainly
there for all to see, writ large in the company's birthchart ...

Astrology can be helpful in even the smallest of companies, not just
for these high street names. For the planets can show you when to
expand and when to stay put; when to retrench and when to preserve
your resources; when to borrow and when to reduce your debts. And
when you should focus on your public image and pay attention to cus-
tomer relations.

In conclusion, financial astrology is essentially concerned with time.
Or to be precise, with how the long and short cycles of time unfold in
the arena of commerce: for, as the experience of the last few years has
so clearly demonstrated, few things in business are more important than
timing. One of the very best ways to time your business and financial
decisions is to study the tools and techniques outlined in this book.
Financial astrology, used correctly, can show you how things are likely
to unfold in the business world, whatever your particular sphere of interest. So if you wish to know what the future holds, there is no better
place to start than with financial astrology – which is, put simply, the
study of cycles.

INTRODUCTION TO ASTROLOGY

Before seeing how financial astrology can be used to formulate predictions for the economy, stock market and individual companies, it will
be necessary for readers to familiarize themselves with some basic astrological concepts. The core principles outlined in this section will be
developed and expanded in the chapters that follow, but it is advisable
to make sure that you have fully understood the ideas contained in these
introductory pages before embarking on the remainder of the book.

We have endeavoured throughout the text to keep astrological jargon to a minimum, but since this *is* a book about how to use the principles of financial astrology in general business and financial forecasting, it would be impossible to convey these ideas without employing some technical language. Although this introduction will furnish you with the all the basic astrology you need to follow the discussion and ideas put forward in this book, we should emphasize that it is by no means all-inclusive. Readers who are interested in learning about the more advanced techniques of financial astrology will find a number of helpful books and courses listed in the Directory of Resources.

FINANCIAL ASTROLOGY: THE BASIC BUILDING BLOCKS

The Planets

Financial astrology can be classified as a form of cyclical analysis and the basic components of the many cycles it uses are the planets. In its broadest sense, the whole science of astrology is concerned with the planets, their relationship with each other and their placement in the zodiac. Financial astrology is the study of how this complex planetary geometry can be applied to business and finance to produce practical, reliable predictions and forecasts.

Our solar system contains nine planets, including the Earth, but as we live on the Earth, astrologers do not include this planet in their calculations. Although technically speaking, the Sun and Moon are not planets, their cycles play such an important role in astrology that for the sake of convenience, they are always included when the term 'planet' is used. In financial astrology, 10 planets are therefore commonly used – the Sun, the Moon and the 8 other planets, excluding the Earth. Unless explicitly stated otherwise, any discussion of 'the planets' should automatically be assumed to include the Sun and Moon.

Planetary Meanings

The following list shows the astrological symbols conventionally used as shorthand for the planets' names, along with their basic definitions. Note that the meanings of the planets in financial astrology differ quite markedly from the meanings attributed to them in natal astrology. This summary provides a simple introduction to the planetary meanings within a financial context, which will be developed in greater depth in Chapter 6.

The Sun ☉

Driving force, a trigger of financial activity and a short-term timing indicator.

The Moon ☽

PERIOD OF ORBIT AROUND THE EARTH: 27½ DAYS

The people, mass markets, public response to events. When combined with the Sun, an important trigger and timing indicator.

Mercury ☿

PERIOD OF ORBIT AROUND THE SUN: 88 DAYS

Trading and commerce in general; trading activity in stock markets. News, communication, travel.

Venus ♀

PERIOD OF ORBIT AROUND THE SUN: 225 DAYS

Money, assets, resources. Popularity and public approval.

Mars ♂

PERIOD OF ORBIT AROUND THE SUN: 1 YEAR 10½ MONTHS

Energy, activity, competitiveness, aggression. Can trigger and augment the size of any market move.

Jupiter ♃

PERIOD OF ORBIT AROUND THE SUN: 12 YEARS

A key business planet. Represents expansion, optimism, moneymaking: the basic symbol of growth.

Saturn ♄

PERIOD OF ORBIT AROUND THE SUN: 29 YEARS

Another key business planet. Represents stability, restriction, pessimism: the basic symbol of contraction.

Uranus ♅

PERIOD OF ORBIT AROUND THE SUN: 84 YEARS

Dynamic innovation and originality. Sudden events, changes and reversals of the status quo.

Neptune Ψ

PERIOD OF ORBIT AROUND THE SUN: 165 YEARS

Idealism, inspiration, or undermining of structures, confusion, illusion and delusion.

Pluto ♇

PERIOD OF ORBIT AROUND THE SUN: 246 YEARS

Power and transformation. Destruction and reconstruction.

The Zodiac

The orbit of the Earth around the Sun defines the plane in which the positions of the planets are measured and this orbital plane is known as the ecliptic. Dividing the 360 degrees of the ecliptic into 12 equal segments produces our second major astrological 'building block' – the 12 signs of the zodiac. We will not discuss the specific meaning of each sign, with the exception of Scorpio (which, as we shall see, plays a key role in stock market analysis). In the main, we will use the signs simply as names for the divisions of the zodiac.

In both astrology and astronomy, the planetary positions are measured from a zero point in the zodiac. This is where the Earth's equator, projected out into space, intersects the Earth's orbital path around the Sun. As seen from the earth, the Sun reaches this zero point (in the northern hemisphere) at the beginning of spring each year, and it is known as 0 degrees Aries, Aries being the first sign of the zodiac.

The Signs of the Zodiac

Listed below are the 12 signs of the zodiac, together with their symbols, and the section of the zodiac that each sign represents.

	Sign	Degree Area		Sign	Degree Area
Aries	♈	0–29	Libra	♎	180–209
Taurus	♉	30–59	Scorpio	♏	210–239
Gemini	♊	60–89	Sagittarius	♐	240–269
Cancer	♋	90–119	Capricorn	♑	270–299
Leo	♌	120–149	Aquarius	♒	300–329
Virgo	♍	150–179	Pisces	♓	330–359

The 12 signs are arranged anti-clockwise in a circle to form the zodiac; this also corresponds to the direction in which the planets move in their orbital paths around the Sun. The signs are also subdivided into three different groups of 'qualities', as follows:

Cardinal: Aries, Cancer, Libra, Capricorn.
Fixed: Taurus, Leo, Scorpio, Aquarius.
Mutable: Gemini, Virgo, Sagittarius, Pisces.

Financial astrologers have found that the qualities correspond to certain clearly defined business attributes. Cardinal signs are associated with pioneering spirit, and drive and initiative in starting new projects. Fixed signs are linked with the qualities of perseverance and staying power, with being able to follow through and make things happen. Mutable signs represent the quality of flexibility, and the ability to adapt to changing times and circumstances.

The Horoscope

Financial astrology also makes use of horoscopes or birthcharts, which can be drawn up for either a country, an institution – such as the UK or US Stock Exchange – or an individual company. Financial horoscopes are based on the same principles as the horoscopes used in natal astrology, with the essential difference that these are charts for organizations rather than individuals and so are subject to some differences in interpretation.

The horoscope is a map of the heavens as seen from Earth, calculated for the exact time, date and place that the particular organization – or nation – came into being. As explained above, the 10 planets used in astrology correspond to certain attributes and qualities, and the planetary arrangement set out in the horoscope – or 'chart', as horoscopes are more commonly called – tells us a great deal about the strengths and weaknesses of its subject. The chart can be analysed to assess the latent potentials that exist within the subject, and also provides a basis upon which predictions about the likely timing of future events or developments can be made. (We will show how this is done in more detail later in this introduction when we take an in-depth look at the UK Stock Exchange chart, which is illustrated in Fig. 1.6, page 26.)

Astrological charts are an essential element in economic and stock market forecasting, as well as investment planning and many other facets of general business management within individual companies.

The Moon's Node

In financial astrology, the position of the Moon's Node is also taken into account. The Node is not a planet, but a point in space, which is formed in the following way. The Moon's orbit around the Earth is not exactly aligned with the ecliptic, but is inclined to it at an angle of 5 degrees 8 minutes. The two points in the Moon's orbit where it cuts the plane of the ecliptic are called the North Node and the South Node. Unless otherwise stated, the Moon's Node is taken to mean the North Node. The Nodes are not static, but move gradually *backwards* around the zodiac, taking 18½ years to complete a full cycle. In 1990, the North Node was in Aquarius; in 1991 it was in Capricorn; in 1992/3 in Sagittarius; and in 1994 and early 1995 it will be in Scorpio. The Moon's Node cycle is particularly relevant to the US economy, as we shall see in Chapters 2 and 3.

The Angles

There are two other pairs of points in the birthchart that are important: the Ascendant–Descendant and the Midheaven–IC. These are known as the angles of the chart. Like the Moon's Node, they are derived from the point of intersection of two planes. As the Earth turns on its axis, the planets appear to rise above the horizon in the east and set in the west. The point where the ecliptic crosses the horizon at any given moment, i.e. the point on the ecliptic that is rising at any given time, is known as the Ascendant. The point directly opposite this, the point on the ecliptic that is setting, is called the Descendant. These two points form the first pair of angles.

The second pair of angles, the Midheaven (MC) and the Imum Coeli (IC), are formed by running a line due north–south through the position of the observer. This line is known as the Meridian. The point where it cuts the ecliptic in the south is called the MC: the point directly opposite it is the IC. At noon local time, the Sun is on the Midheaven; at midnight local time, it is on the IC.

When a planet in the birthchart is positioned close to an angle, its effect is emphasized and will tend to be more powerfully felt. This also applies to transits, for when transiting planets cross the angles of a birthchart, the transit generally manifests as some kind of event.

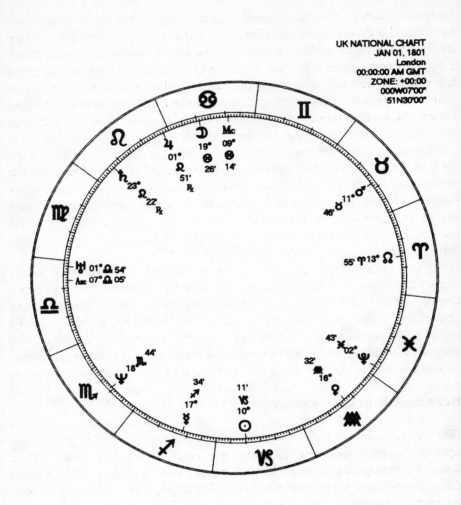

FIGURE 1.1: UK NATIONAL CHART

Transits

To make financial forecasts, two major techniques are used. Firstly, we can take the positions of the planets at a given time and see how they interact with the natal planetary positions, which are shown in the chart. The positions of the planets at a given time are known in astrology as transits, and can tell us a great deal about what will be happening at that time. We will explore exactly how transits operate in greater detail later in the section when we come to look at national and stock exchange charts.

A second predictive approach widely used in financial astrology is to look at the relationships between the transiting planets themselves. We do this by calculating the horoscope for a given moment, which provides us with a key to the underlying trends that may be present. As we shall see in later chapters, when transiting planets form important symmetric patterns with each other, these configurations can have an important effect on the economy or on the stock market.

There is a significant difference between these two methods of working with transits that should be noted. Whereas the first method takes the positions of the transiting planets and applies them to a company, national or stock exchange chart to give localized indications of likely events, the second approach – analysing the interrelationships of the transiting planets between themselves – can provide us with a global picture, which is not tied in to any individual organization or country.

Heliocentric and Geocentric Positions

The charts or horoscopes used in financial astrology are generally set up from an Earth-centred, or geocentric, perspective, for it is a central tenet of astrology that in order to understand and predict events on Earth, the planetary positions must be analysed from this point of view. However, for certain purposes, such as making predictions of economic activity, it has been found useful to use the positions and aspects between the planets as seen from the Sun, rather than the Earth. These are known as heliocentric, or Sun-centred, positions.

In general, geocentric positions have been found to be useful for charting short-term effects, such as movements in the stock market or individual company work, whereas heliocentric positions are more relevant to understanding the longer-term movements of the economy.

The Retrograde Effect

Observed from a Sun-centred, heliocentric perspective, the planets always move forwards in their orbits, but when viewed geocentrically, there are certain times when they appear to stop and move backwards. In astrology this is known as retrograde motion. To understand why this occurs, we will first consider what happens in the case of the inner planets Mercury and Venus.

Fig. 1.2 shows the positions of Venus and the Earth on three separate dates, when Venus – which moves faster than the Earth – is on the opposite side of the Sun from the Earth. Viewed from the Earth, Venus moves forward, or anticlockwise, in the zodiac; this is called direct motion. In Fig. 1.3, Venus is on the same side of the Sun as the Earth and, since it moves faster in its orbit than the Earth, overtakes it. Seen from the Earth, Venus appears to be moving backwards at this time. When this apparent backward motion occurs, Venus is said to be retrograde.

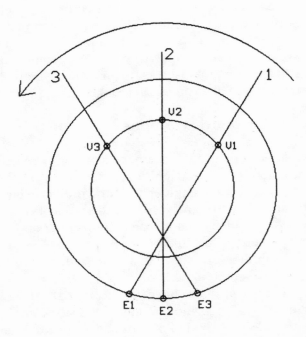

FIGURE 1.2

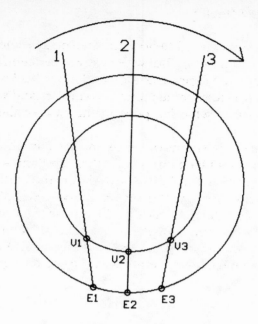

FIGURE 1.3

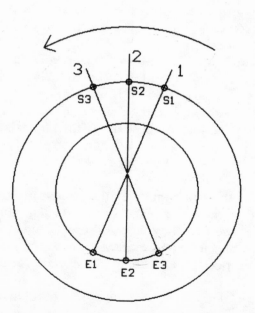

FIGURE 1.4

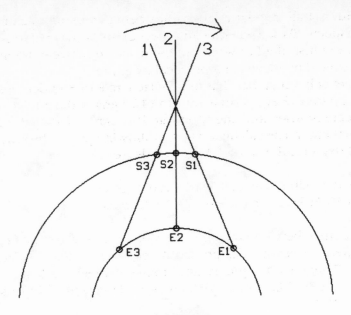

FIGURE 1.5

A similar situation occurs with the planets that lie beyond the Earth. Fig. 1.4 depicts Saturn on the opposite side of the Sun to the Earth; here Saturn is moving forward in the zodiac, in direct motion. When the Earth and Saturn are on the same side as the Sun, as in Fig. 1.5, the Earth – which moves faster than Saturn – overtakes it, and Saturn seems to be moving backwards, i.e. retrograde. The times when a planet changes from direct to retrograde motion, or from retrograde to direct – that is, when it appears to stop and change direction – are very important, as we will see in later chapters. At these times, the planet is said to 'station'.

The Aspects

When we consider the arrangement of the planets in a birthchart, or the relationship that the transiting planets have to each other at any particular moment, we see that they lie at different angular distances from each other within the circle of the horoscope. These planetary relationships, known as aspects, are extremely important for predicting likely future events.

Aspects are crucial to fine-tuning the timing of financial events in the economy, the stock market and also within individual companies, and are therefore one of the major factors we shall be considering in this book. But not all angular relationships between planets can be classified as aspects. To see whether an aspect exists between two planets, it is necessary first of all to work out the distance between them. This is best illustrated by means of a practical example.

Readers will remember that the zodiac circle of 360 degrees can be divided up into 12 equal segments, the 12 signs of the zodiac. If Sun is at 10 degrees Aries and the Moon at 10 degrees Libra, the distance between them can be calculated in the following way. (The start of Libra is at 180 degrees; the start of Aries at 0 degrees.)

Moon at 10 Libra   = 10 + 180 = 190 degrees
Sun at 10 Aries   = 10 + 0   = 10 degrees

The distance between the Sun and Moon is therefore 180 degrees.

Considering a second example, if Mercury is at 5 degrees Taurus and Jupiter at 7 degrees Leo, the distance between them is calculated as follows. (The start of Leo is at 120 degrees, and the start of Taurus is at 30 degrees.)

Mercury at 7 Leo   = 7 + 120 = 127 degrees
Jupiter at 5 Taurus = 5 + 30   = 35 degrees

The distance between Mercury and Jupiter is therefore 92 degrees.

Major Aspects

In astrological analysis, we find that certain angular relationships between the planets tend to produce clear effects, and these are, therefore, significant for forecasting purposes. These angular distances – or aspects – result from the division of the circle of 360 degrees by small whole numbers. The principal aspects which are used in natal astrology as well as financial astrology are called the major aspects, and these are calculated as follows:

Aspect Name	Symbol	Divide Circle by	Angle
Conjunction	☌	1	0 (or 360)
Opposition	☍	2	180
Trine	△	3	120 and 240
Square	□	4	90 and 270
Sextile	✳	6	60 and 300

The conjunction occurs when two planets are in the same place; the opposition when they are 180 degrees apart, i.e. opposite each other. The remaining aspects can all occur at two separate places within the circle. For example, the Moon can make a trine to the Sun by being 120 degrees ahead of the Sun or by being 120 degrees behind it. Note that 120 degrees behind is the same as 240 degrees ahead:

$$120 + 240 = 360$$

Similarly, the square and sextile also have two positions in which the aspect occurs.

In general terms, the conjunction, square and opposition are classified as 'hard' or 'challenging' aspects, as they have been found to produce testing or difficult effects. The trine and sextile, on the other hand, are known as 'soft' or 'flowing' aspects, and generally denote more favourable results. These are very broad definitions, however, and although these tend to hold true for the economy and the stock market, they do not apply across the board. In company astrology, as we shall see, the interpretation of aspects is more complex.

In financial astrology, the meaning of any given aspect is derived from the nature of the particular planets involved, e.g. a Moon–Pluto conjunction or a Sun–Mars opposition. These individual meanings will be explained in full in the relevant sections of each chapter.

Orbs

Aspects produce significant effects not simply when the aspect relationship is exact, but also during the period when the two planets are a small distance from the exact aspect. As the planets move closer and closer towards creating the exact aspect, the aspect strength increases; as the planets move apart, the aspect strength decreases. This difference between the actual angle between two planets and the exact aspect angle is known as the orb of the aspect. The smaller the orb, the closer the aspect is to being exact and the more powerful the effect.

In subsequent chapters, we will occasionally look at important aspects which are up to 5 degrees from being exact, as this is the point at which aspects begin to produce observable effects. But when the orbs are reduced to 1 or 2 degrees, the effects become much stronger and such close aspects are, therefore, by far the most important.

Returning to our previous examples, we can see that in the first instance, the difference between the Sun and Moon was 180 degrees: the planets were therefore making an exact opposition to each other, and the orb of the aspect was therefore zero. In the second example, Mercury and Jupiter were 92 degrees apart and were therefore 2 degrees from being in exact square to each other. The orb of the square in this case was 2 degrees.

Minor Aspects

In addition to the major aspects listed above, astrologers also make use of several 'minor' aspects, so-called because although they give rise to perceptible effects, they are not as striking as those produced by the major aspects. Like the major aspects, minor aspects are formed by dividing the circle of 360 degrees by whole numbers. The most important minor aspects to note are:

Aspect	Divide circle by	Angle
Semisquare	8	45 and 315
Sesquisquare	8	135 and 225
Quintile	5	72, 144, 216, 288

The semisquare and sesquisquare are both derived from one-eighth of a circle, the semisquare being ⅛th, and the sesquisquare being ⅜th of the circle. Both these aspects tend to produce stressful or difficult effects, or can act as triggers for other aspects. The quintile is generally viewed as a positive influence.

The Ephemeris

If you intend to incorporate astrological techniques into your financial decision-making, it is essential to have some means of knowing where the planets are on any given day. There are two sources for this information. You can either choose one of the various computer programmes currently on the market or you can use an ephemeris.

An ephemeris (plural: ephemerides) shows the positions of the planets on each day and is available in computer or book form. Printed ephemerides are issued for individual years and also in volumes that cover the whole of this century. At first glance, the ephemeris can look rather daunting, as it consists entirely of printed columns of figures and symbols, but with practice, you will soon find it easy to use. An ephemeris is an extremely useful resource to have on hand when you wish to quickly assess how the planets are moving and the aspect patterns that will be in operation over a particular period of time. The Directory of Resources lists a number of good ephemeris books, plus contact addresses for suppliers of astrological computer software.

As astrological charts are calculated from a geocentric perspective, the most widely used ephemerides give geocentric positions. These have been found to be the most useful positions for stock market and company work; heliocentric ephemerides are also available. As well as planetary positions, an ephemeris will give you the exact time for New Moons, Full Moons, and First and Last Quarters each month, as well as information on solar and lunar eclipses. Such data are essential for predicting stock market movements and in company work, as we shall see in Chapters 5 and 6.

ASTROLOGY AND CYCLES

Astrologically based cycles analysis allows us to predict the peaks and troughs of the business cycle, as well as to forecast the times when the stock market is likely to be bullish or bearish. Using this cyclical approach also allows us to assess the best times for expansion or consolidation within a company and assess the potential of any given company as an investment vehicle.

So what exactly are these planetary cycles and how do they operate? The cycles used in financial astrology relate to the planets and the Node. The movement of a planet through the zodiac from 0 degrees Aries through Taurus, Gemini etc. and back to 0 degrees Aries forms a cycle, just as the Sun moving round the zodiac produces the cycle of the year's seasons. In addition, financial astrology uses the cycles between two planets. For example, the Jupiter–Saturn cycle begins conventionally when the two planets are in conjunction and as Jupiter moves faster than Saturn, over time Jupiter will move through all the aspects to Saturn before returning to the conjunction; a process that takes about 20 years.

Like aspects, cycles describe the relationship that exists between two planets. But whereas aspects convey this information in a static, structural way, cycles provide a more dynamic, moving model of the same planetary relationship. A good way of illustrating this essential difference between aspects and cycles is to think of a cycle as a continuous video film of a particular process at work in the economy or markets, rising and falling over time. Using the same analogy, if we stop the video at certain key points, e.g., when the planets are at 90, 180 or 120 degrees to each other, and 'freeze-frame', what we get is an aspect. So whereas the Jupiter–Saturn cycle, for example, corresponds to the whole film, a

Jupiter–Saturn aspect, such as a square or a trine, is like a still photograph of a single point in the process.

When charting the potential movements of either the economy or the stock market, it is crucial to consider both cycles and aspects, for each provides vital information about the likely pattern of events. In general, cycles give a good background picture of what will be happening at any given time: the broad brush-strokes of the business cycle or the market. Aspects, on the other hand, provide us with the precise timing that is essential for formulating forecasts and predictions. By using aspects, we can work out the precise day, and sometimes even the precise *time*, when, for example, the stock market will turn. The effects produced by the business and financial planetary cycles vary, some affecting the economy, others primarily the stock market, and this is best illustrated by two key examples.

Historically, the most important cycle that has been identified as a determinant of recession and growth in the economy is the 20-year Jupiter–Saturn cycle. This cycle, formed by the interaction of these two major business planets, has been shown by financial astrologers to have been a major causal factor in not only the profound recession of the 1990s, but also the Great Depression and in many other major business downturns that have occurred since 1810.

A different range of cycles affects the stock market and research has shown that one of the most crucial cycles here is the Saturn–Pluto cycle. As we shall see in Chapter 4, the square aspect of this cycle produces severe falls in the UK market. The same cycle also operates in the US market, but this time, it is the opposition aspect that is followed by serious falls.

Incidentally, both the Jupiter–Saturn cycle and the Saturn–Pluto cycle are slow-moving ones which need to be activated or 'triggered' by faster-moving cycles. How this process works will be fully explained in Chapters 3 and 4.

Irregular Financial Cycles

One of the major advantages that financial astrology offers as a method of forecasting is its ability to explain and predict irregular cycles in the economy and financial markets. All the work that has hitherto been carried out on financial cycles by economists and market analysts has tended to focus on fixed-length cycles, such as the 20-year or 34-month cycles identified in the economy and the stock market. These cycles are expected to repeat with exactly the same timing and so researchers assume that the stock market will peak every 34 months or that there will be a recession every 20 years. Unfortunately researchers working in this way have no alternative to such fixed length cycles. They have no systematic reason to expect one occurrence of the cycle to be longer or shorter than the last and certainly do not have any way of predicting in advance when a cycle will be shorter or longer than its average length.

Astrology provides a more flexible and powerful approach. Because it introduces an external factor – the cycles of the planets – its cycles can be predicted in advance and the astrological cycle between two planets does not take the same amount of time on each occasion that it occurs. This provides forecasters with the possibility of slightly different cycle lengths for each occurrence of the cycle. The following example will help to make this clear:

In Chapter 4, we will be looking at the effect that the Venus cycle has on the stock market. When viewed geocentrically, Venus does not move at a constant speed, but from time to time slows down, stops, appears to move backwards, stops and then resumes its direct motion. Over a period of time, the Venus cycle from 0 degrees Aries back to 0 degrees Aries averages out at one year, but each individual cycle may take more or less than a year, as shown below:

Venus at 0 Aries	Length of Venus cycle
22 April 1987	
	293 days
9 February 1988	
	408 days
23 March 1989	
	346 days
4 March 1990	
	355 days
22 February 1991	
	410 days
7 April 1992	
	301 days
2 February 1993	

Clearly, the length of the Venus zodiac cycle varies greatly and were we to combine the Venus cycle with another planetary cycle, such as Mars, the resulting cycle would be even more variable. On average, over a long period of time, the cycle length would average out to a particular value, but using this average length for the cycle as a fixed length would produce very bad timing mistakes if the market were really responding to the variable astrological cycle.

The conventional use of fixed cycle lengths may 'seem' to work over a period, but often the peaks and troughs in the theoretical cycle do not accurately time the actual peaks and troughs in the market. Forecasters working with the variable length astrological cycles, however, have found that they do provide an answer to this difficult problem and allow them accurately to determine the length of any particular instance of a cycle well in advance.

National and Stock Exchange Charts

National and stock exchange charts are important tools that can be used to assess the likely impact of transiting planetary configurations. For if an aspect between transiting planets links in strongly with one of these charts, its effect on either the stock market or the economy will be stronger and more pronounced.

Earlier we saw how charts for individual nations and institutions, like the stock exchange, can be set up using the date, time and place at which they came into being. National charts play a very important role in determining the precise turning-points of the economy in individual countries and these will be examined in greater detail in Chapter 3, 'Predicting the Economy'.

No introduction to financial astrology would be complete without an interpretation of a horoscope, however, and so we will conclude this section by taking a brief look at another important chart, that of the UK Stock Exchange.

Fig. 1.6. shows a chart set up for the date and time of the legal foundation of the UK Stock Exchange. Around the outer edge of the circle are the signs of the zodiac. Within the circle is a diagrammatic representation of how the planets were arranged on that day, as seen from Earth.

If we quickly review our planetary symbols, we can see that near the top of the chart lies Jupiter, which is placed at 26 degrees and 48 minutes of Leo. Five degrees further on lies Saturn at 1 degree 48 minutes of Virgo. The retrograde symbol ℞ placed beneath both Jupiter and Saturn means that on the day that the stock exchange was 'born', both Jupiter and Saturn were moving retrograde as seen from Earth.

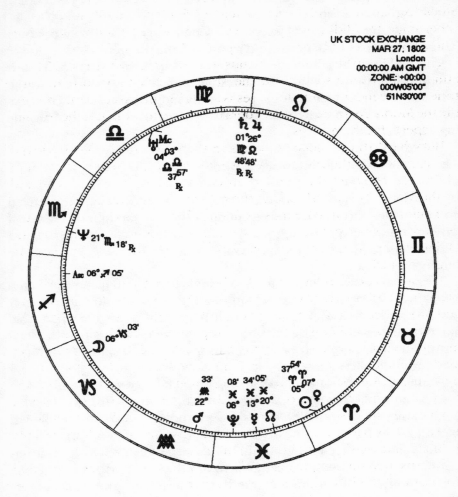

FIGURE 1.6: UK STOCK EXCHANGE

On the left of the chart, at about 'nine o'clock', lies the symbol for one of the angles, the Ascendant (ASC), which in the case of the UK Stock Exchange (UKSE) falls at 6 degrees 5 minutes of Sagittarius. The other angle, the Midheaven, is always found towards the top of the chart. The UKSE has a Midheaven of 3 degrees 57 minutes of Libra.

The UKSE has the Sun and Venus in conjunction in Aries. Both the Sun and Venus are squared by the Moon in early Capricorn and also trine the Ascendant. Pluto in Pisces is square to the Ascendant and sextile the Moon. As an exercise, readers might like to work out the remaining aspects for themselves.

But what do the planetary symbols and aspects actually mean? A major aspect pattern in the UK Stock Exchange chart is the very close pattern of Uranus conjunct the Midheaven opposition Venus, both squared by the Moon. This clearly shows the role of a stock exchange, whereby free enterprise (Uranus) builds its financial resources (Venus) from the general investing public (the Moon). The position of Uranus on the Midheaven (goals and objectives) emphasizes the free enterprise nature of the market.

This aspect pattern has proved to be sensitive to transits. For example, when Jupiter (the planet of expansion) passed over the Midheaven and proceeded to activate the pattern in July and August 1981, the market rose. Again, in November 1992, Jupiter transiting over this point moved the market up. After moving backwards over the pattern, Jupiter made its final pass of this cycle in June 1993, again pushing the market upwards. Readers should note that one planet activating the pattern will not produce major moves on its own, but it can set a background trend – which, in the case of Jupiter will of course be a bullish (expansionary) one. This pattern was also part of the astrological build-up to Black Monday and we will look at this in more detail in Chapter 5.

We trust that this simple introduction to astrology will have provided you with all the basic building blocks you need in order to make the most of *Money and the Markets*. We suggest that readers who are totally new to astrology should review the foregoing sections and ensure that they have understood them thoroughly before proceeding with the rest of the book.

References

1. Houston W., *Meltdown*, Smith Gryphon, 1993.
2. Rees-Mogg W. & Davidson J., *The Great Reckoning*, Sidgwick & Jackson, London, 1992, p.228.

Financial Astrology: An Historical Overview

From the earliest days of recorded history, man has used the principles and insights of astrology to help guide his actions and decision-making in all areas of daily life, including finance and commerce. The specialist discipline of financial astrology, however, is a relatively recent one which has largely come into existence over the last two centuries. The main landmarks in the development of financial astrology as a forecasting tool are essentially contemporaneous with the explosion in business activity that accompanied the emergence of the Western nations as industrial powers in the wake of the Industrial Revolution. In the following pages, we will survey the main developments in financial astrology up to the 1980s, when this specialist discipline was suddenly transformed out of all recognition by the revolution which took place in information technology.

Prior to the late eighteenth and early nineteenth centuries, the global economy was predominantly agricultural in nature. Economic cycles were synonymous with the fluctuating rhythms of good and bad harvests, the years of plenty and famine. When the Western world's centuries old dependence on wood and water gave way to an economy based on coal and iron, and the population began its inexorable drift from the countryside into the towns, the commercial sector began to develop in parallel. A new class of businessman began to emerge; and with the growth of this new entrepreneurial spirit, there arose a corresponding interest in forecasting the ups and downs of the 'business cycle'.

Since the transition from a rural economy to an industrial one was a gradual process which took place over several decades, a major part of business activity in the early nineteenth century was still focused around the production of crops. Much of the early financial forecasting work was concerned, therefore, with attempting to explain fluctuations in agricultural production, in particular the price of grain. Astrological axioms and laws had been in use almost continuously since early times to help predict the weather and the harvests, and constituted an early form of forecasting. But in keeping with the scientific fashions of the day, a parallel field of scientific inquiry sprang up during the eighteenth, nineteenth and early twentieth centuries that sought to arrive at a more mechanistic explanation of terrestrial events. As this research has so many points of contact with astrology, it is worth exploring in some detail before going on to consider the work of the early financial astrologers.

The eminent English astronomer Sir William Herschel, best known for his discovery of the planet Uranus in 1781, was one of the first to put forward an hypothesis to explain the ebbs and flows of the business cycle. This hypothesis was destined to fascinate researchers for generations to come – and came to be known as the 'sunspot theory'.

THE BEGINNINGS OF CYCLES ANALYSIS: THE SUNSPOT CYCLE

In 1801 Herschel read a paper before the Royal Society in London in which he drew attention to the apparent relationship between sunspots and the price of wheat.[1] During periods of low sunspot activity, he noted that the wheat harvest was poor and the price consequently high. During periods of high sunspot activity, however, the wheat harvest was good and prices fell. Herschel's observations were soon borne out by experience, as the four years from 1809 to 1812 were marked by low sunspot activity and rising prices for wheat. It is now a well established and widely accepted scientific fact that all kinds of plant life are more abundant in times of heavy sunspot activity. Although the earliest records of sunspot observation are contained in the great Chinese *Encyclopaedia* of 1322, which lists 45 observations of sunspots between 301 and 1205 AD, and Galileo and his contemporaries began their scientific studies of sunspots in 1610, Herschel was one of the first astronomers to perceive the correspondence between the sunspot cycle and the behaviour of particular commodities.

A few words of general explanation about sunspots will be helpful at this point. Although sunspots have long been known to exert a noticeable influence on events on Earth, the mechanism underlying the formation of sunspots, and the reason why their abundance or scarcity is cyclical, remains a mystery. Sunspots are basically dark patches or spots that appear on the surface of the sun and are slightly cooler than the surrounding area. They are transitory and fleeting; an individual spot may last no longer than three or perhaps four weeks in total. The number of spots visible to astronomers varies over time in a cycle of approximately 11 years. The cycle begins with very few spots, then builds to a maximum formation about five or six years later, and subsequently dies down again. Although the average period of the cycle is 11.1 years, it is important to note that individual cycles can range in length from 8 to 16 years.

The sunspot cycle is a complex phenomenon, however, and scientists and astronomers are still far from fully understanding its erratic behaviour. What appears to be a simple cycle is in fact a double cycle of twice the apparent length. Sunspots always form in pairs, each being of opposite magnetic polarity. It has been found that the apparent 11-year cycle is in fact a 22-year cycle, with a polarity reversal at the halfway point. Given the unexplained origins of the sunspot cycle and its influence on terrestrial events, the challenge of delineating the precise character of the relationship between solar activity and economic fluctuations was one which fascinated several theoreticians in the decades following Herschel's initial research.

The next researcher to formulate a coherent theory linking sunspots and the business cycle was the English economist W. S. Jevons. In 1875 he read a paper before the Bristol meeting of the British Association for the Advancement of Science entitled 'The Solar Period and the Price of Corn'[2] in which he noted an 11-year cycle in the general level of prices, which he related to the sunspot cycle in the following words:

> Assuming that variations of commercial credit and enterprise are essentially mental in nature, must there not be external events to excite hopefulness at one time or disappointment and despondency at another? It may be that the commercial classes of the English nation, as at present constituted, form a body, suited by mental and other conditions, to go through a complete oscillation in a period nearly corresponding to that of the sunspots. In such conditions, a comparatively slight variation of the prices of food, repeated in a similar manner, at corresponding points in the oscillation, would suffice to produce violent effects.

After reviewing the possibility that the sunspot cycle is somehow linked to planetary orbits, Jevons makes the following statement (our emphasis):

> Now, if the planets govern the Sun, and the Sun governs the vintages and harvests, and thus the price of food and raw materials, and the state of the money market, it follows that *the configuration of the planets may prove to be the remote causes of the greatest commercial disasters*.

The sunspot theory waned in popularity during the late Victorian era, when it was generally dismissed by contemporary economists although, it must be said, they had little better to offer as a predictive tool. It resurfaced during the troubled years of the 1930s when theorists and policy-makers throughout the Western world were desperately searching for formulas that could explain the persistent malaise of the global economy. In November 1934 Dr C. Garcia-Mata and Dr F. I. Shaffner published a paper[3] reporting the results of their investigation into links between the behaviour of the sun and business cycles. When they examined total production in the USA – excluding agriculture – for the period 1875 to 1930, they found a very high correlation between solar activity and total manufacturing production. Curiously, the two researchers also found that the link between crop yields and the sunspot cycle which Herschel had detected over a century earlier was now far less pronounced. But since agriculture no longer played such a dominant role in the economy, the link was no longer relevant. So instead of sunspots affecting the weather (and by implication crop yields), thereby influencing the general level of prices, the scenario pieced together by the researchers of the 1930s led to the conclusion that sunspots could now be directly correlated with economic activity itself.

While economists hoped that the sunspot theory might hold the key to predicting economic fluctuations, astronomers were still preoccupied with the question of why the sunspot cycle existed in the first place. Their investigations were also highly pertinent to understanding business fluctuations, for if the astronomers could discover what caused the sunspot cycle and were able to predict it, and the sunspot cycle was proven to affect the level of economic activity, then those same factors would clearly have a role to play in determining the pattern of the business cycle.

In 1863, the English astronomer R. C. Carrington published his *Observations of Spots on the Sun*,[4] which featured a chart showing the correlation between the sunspot cycle and the distance of the planet Jupiter from the Sun, which has a period of 11.86 years. Although the correlation was not very pronounced, Carrington's study was important as it was among the first to recognise the possibility that the planets of the solar system might in some way modulate the behaviour of the Sun, and so cause the sunspot cycle. Following on from Carrington's work, the astronomer Professor W. A. Norton of Yale observed in his book *A Treatise on Astronomy* (1867):[5]

> The sun's spots are for the most part developed by, or in some way connected with, the operation of a physical agency exerted by the planets upon the photosphere ... the planets which exercise the greatest influence are Jupiter and Venus ... It appears from the results of observation, *that the planets operate unequally in different parts of the ecliptic, and in different relative positions ...*' (our emphasis)

Norton's observations suggest a clear link to astrology, in that the 'different parts of the ecliptic' correspond to the division of the ecliptic into astrological signs, and the 'different relative positions' is another way of describing the astrologer's aspects. Over the next few years, several other planets were seen to play a causal role in sunspot formation. In 1869–70, the English astronomers De La Rue, Stewart and Loewy, writing in *Researches on Solar Physics*,[6] postulated that not only were Jupiter and Venus involved in sunspot formation, but also that the relationship of Venus to Mercury, Mars to Jupiter and the zodiac position of Mercury all made contributions. Astronomers and economists alike were forced to acknowledge that there was no simple answer to be found to the question of what caused the sunspot cycle and that the whole mechanism was far more complicated than had originally been suspected.

The theories put forward by astronomers to explain the cycle thus grew increasingly complex. In his paper, 'A Possible Explanation of the Sunspot Period' published in 1900 in the *Monthly Notices* of the Royal Astronomical Society,[7] Professor E. W. Brown of Yale looked further afield than his predecessors to consider the effects of the angular relationship – astrologically speaking, the aspect – between the planets Jupiter and Saturn, and its correlation with the sunspot cycle. This study in particular has interesting implications for the later work of financial astrologers, since Jupiter and Saturn are often called 'the business planets', and their cycles have since been irrefutably shown to be linked with the business cycle.

Research into the sunspot cycle has continued up to the present day, and many recent studies have confirmed the earlier hypotheses that not just Jupiter but several other planets are involved in the cycle's mechanism. In 1953, Professor C. J. Bollinger, writing in the *Atlas of Planetary and Solar Climate*,[8] showed that there is a consistent relationship between the sunspot cycle and the configuration of Jupiter, Venus and the Earth. The scientific journal *Nature* for 10 November 1972[9] carried an article by K. D. Wood of the University of Colorado, who used the tidal effect on the sun of Mercury, Venus, the Earth and Jupiter to construct a very tight match to the sunspot cycle for the period 1800 to 1972. Particularly interesting is the forecast that Wood produced, based on this research, for the next two cycles leading up to the year 2000. So far, these predictions for the behaviour of the most recent sunspot cycles seem to have provided an accurate match with what has actually happened.

By the mid-nineteenth century, other fields of inquiry were opening up. Researchers working in the field of financial forecasting were beginning to conclude that not only the sunspot cycle but also the planetary

positions themselves might hold the key to explaining the cyclical fluctuations of the economy. In addition to the 8–16-year sunspot cycle, the
Victorian researchers were also beginning to perceive that there were other
distinct rhythms that could be observed at work in the economy and the
study of the business cycle *per se* became a growing preoccupation.

CYCLES RESEARCH: THE EARLY YEARS

The Victorians had the best possible motive for wishing to predict the
workings of the business cycle, for it was during the nineteenth century
that investing and speculating on the stock market became a firmly established feature of commercial life. Although the first joint-stock company
was established in England in 1553, when the Muscovy Company – more
properly known as 'The Mysterie and Companie of Merchant Adventurers
for the Discoverie of Regions, Dominions, Islands and Places Unknowen'
– was founded to finance the voyages of the explorer Sebastian Cabot,
stock market speculation did not become a mainstream business activity until after 1800. The main catalyst for the expansion of joint-stock
companies was the railway boom. The exorbitant capital costs involved
in railway construction were too large to be borne by individual fami-
lies and partnerships alone, and funds had be raised further afield. Following
the opening of the first public railway from Stockton to Darlington in
1825, 'Railway Fever' gripped the country, and railway promoters took
advantage of this newfound enthusiasm by persuading thousands of
middle and upper-class speculators to invest their savings in the new
listed companies.

The memory of the 1720 'South Seas Bubble', when thousands of
people had lost all their savings in a cataclysmic crash – and even such distinguished individuals as Sir Isaac Newton had lost substantial sums – was
deeply ingrained in the national psyche. Since the Victorian speculators
were not anxious to repeat the mistakes of their forefathers, interest in charting the ups and downs of the market grew rapidly at this time. Following
a further speculative flurry in 1825, researchers began to gather information in an attempt to see whether a pattern to the stock market cycle could
be observed. The English statistician Dr H. Clark, writing in Herapath's
Railway Magazine of 1838,[10] a prime source of information for investors
in the railway boom, observed periods of speculation running in 10-, 13-
and 14-year cycles. In the *Railway Register* of 1847,[11] he subsequently identified a cycle of famines and panics of between 10 and 11 years, which
served to further confirm Herschel's work and anticipated Jevons's correlation of this economic pattern with the sunspot cycle.

As economists and statisticians gathered more and more information on the modulations of economic activity, other cycles began to be identified, and several of these early discoveries are now recognised as being highly significant for forecasting purposes. In 1860 Clement Juglar, a French economist, showed that trade fluctuations were cyclical and postulated that a major cycle existed with a period of nine years; this is still known as 'the Juglar cycle'. Sixty-three years later, the American economist Joseph Kitchin announced his discovery of a three-and-a-third-year cycle (40 months) in US and UK statistics for the period 1890–1922.[12] Kitchin based his findings on an exhaustive study of three different series of data for both countries: commodity prices, interest rates and bank clearings – all of which give clear indications as to the general level of economic activity. Kitchin's cycle is now recognised as being very significant and he also formulated the crucial theory that major long-term cycles are formed as sub-harmonics of this 40-month cycle. When every second cycle is emphasised, the result is an 80-month or seven-year cycle. This theory of sub-harmonic cycles is extremely important and we will explore it in greater detail in later chapters of this book.

One of the best known analyses of price cycles over a long period of time is that of the UK statistician W. H. Beveridge. This also provides one of the closest correlations with astrological cycles. Beveridge's famous study of the price of wheat in Western Europe, based on 300 years of data spanning the period from 1544 to 1844, was published in two papers in 1921[13] and 1922.[14] In this study, he identified several different cycles of varying length, including 3.41 years, which matches the Kitchin cycle, and 11 years, which correlates to the sunspot cycle, as well as several other cycles whose periods correspond very closely to those of various astrological cycles, including the following:

Beveridge Period	Astrological Cycle and Period
5.96 years	Half-orbital period of Jupiter 5.93 years
9.75 years	Third orbital period of Saturn 9.82 years
12.84 years	Jupiter–Neptune cycle 12.78 years
19.9 years	Jupiter–Saturn cycle 19.86 years
35.5 years	Saturn–Neptune cycle 35.87 years

It is worth noting that over the whole 300 years of the data, none of these astrological cycles differs from Beveridge's cycles by more than a quarter of a cycle.

The interest in charting cycles and all their variations continues unabated to the present day, and one of the most assiduous researchers of the century, indeed of all time, is the American Edward Dewey. In 1941 he set up the Foundation for the Study of Cycles, a group that still actively collects and disseminates information on cycles occurring in the economy and markets, as well as weather cycles and natural phenomena. Dewey's work includes research on the planetary causes of sunspots, business cycles and stock market cycles. The Foundation publishes a monthly newsletter, *Cycles*, which features articles and reports on its latest findings. (For further details about the Foundation and its publications, see the Directory of Resources at the back of the book.) A full review of Dewey's work and the subsequent work of the Foundation would require a book in itself, and interested readers should contact the Foundation for further information.

One piece of work by Dewey is particularly relevant, as it highlights one of the problems researchers face when attempting to pinpoint economic and market cycles. In the December 1965 issue of *Cycles*, Dewey put forward evidence for 37 possible cycles in the US stock market observed during the period 1937–65. These cycles ranged in length from 30 months up to nearly 11 years. In particular he isolated periods of 9.2 years (which is similar to the Juglar business cycle) and 38 months. This 38-month cycle identified by Dewey is similar to the 40-month Kitchin cycle. Interestingly, there also appears to be evidence in other economic and market studies for a periodic fluctuation of around this length, some researchers reporting a short Dewey-style period of 38 months, others a longer period ranging up to 42 months, depending on the particular economic or market series being studied, and the time span of the data used in the research. Researchers seeking to use cycles of economic activity to construct accurate models for financial forecasting can run into major problems when cycles are irregular, and appear to either change length or have a slightly different period, depending on the economic series being studied. Fortunately, as we saw in Chapter 1, financial astrology can generally explain what is happening in such cases, since the fluctuations of these irregular cycles can generally be explained by astrological cycles, rather than the fixed-length cycles generally used by economists.

Dewey's identification of a 9.2-year Juglar-style cycle was confirmed by James Vaux, writing in the May 1976 issue of *Cycles*, where he updated Dewey's work using the Standard and Poor 500 index. Vaux found the cycle to be 9.22 years long and very reliable. The theoretical peaks and troughs he posited after 1976 were a low in mid-1978, a high in early 1983 and a low in late 1987! The next high was due in mid-1992 and next low at the end of 1996...

Before looking at the work of astrologers on the business cycle and stock markets, we should mention what is perhaps the best known (but also the least clearly defined) economic cycle. In 1926, after a detailed study of American economic affairs, the Russian economist Kondratieff put forward the theory that there is a long-term cycle at work in business with a period ranging from 47 to 60 years. Since a great deal of uncertainty surrounded the length of this cycle, a lively debate ensued as to whether it actually existed at all. Sadly, the Soviet authorities took a dim view of Kondratieff's work and he was exiled to Siberia before he had the opportunity to refine his hypothesis further – since his theory contradicted the Marxist doctrine that capitalism was on a downward path and would eventually self-destruct!

Kondratieff's work does, however, serve to highlight a fundamental problem implicit in any work involving the study of long-term cycles. Although the concept of the business cycle has changed out of all recognition since the Industrial Revolution, it is easy to forget that there have in fact only been three *complete* cycles of 50 years from 1800 up until the present day. When considered from the perspective of all the other cycles which are simultaneously unfolding and interacting, it is hardly surprising that the exact period of these longer cycles has been so hard to establish. It has also proved equally difficult to determine the long-term cycles operating in the stock market, for similar reasons.

FINANCIAL ASTROLOGY: THE PIONEERS

Many of the cycles identified by the early researchers in the field of economics were already well known in general terms to astrologers, since they corresponded, with great accuracy, to known planetary cycles. It still remained, however, for this knowledge to be systematically applied to business. Apart from the perennial trade in astrological almanacs, which continued to offer predictions on harvests, the weather and other miscellaneous topics, the nineteenth century was a period during which astrology remained, for the most part, relatively obscure. But by the 1900s there was a small but growing group of stock market analysts who were utilising its ancient laws for handsome financial gain. The most famous of these early proponents of financial astrology was W. D. Gann.

Born on a ranch in Texas in 1878, Gann is often considered to be the 'patron saint' of financial astrologers, but is best known in business circles for his work in the field of technical analysis. He began his working life as a cotton warehouse clerk, but had soon shrugged off his humble origins to become a Wall Street legend. During a career that spanned half a century, Gann pulled over $50 million from the stock and commodity markets by his uncanny ability to predict exactly how the markets would behave and, more importantly, when they would turn. So impressive was his success rate that by 1910 he was offering a consultancy service that cost around $3,000 to $4,000 per year, at a time when the average American wage was only about $60 per month. Starting on 1 October 1909, Gann gave a public demonstration of his trading skills. In front of a group of reporters and witnesses, he made 286 trades during a 25-day period, of which a staggering 254 were profitable. This gave him a 92 per cent success rate! It must be assumed, however, that Gann did not select the particular 25-day period at random and as his trading marathon was well-publicised in the national press, it was a highly effective public relations exercise too.

Gann was a fascinating and complex character. Deeply religious, he was a patient, disciplined trader with a highly unorthodox, at times maverick, way of working. He was painstakingly thorough, and laboriously researched the prices of stocks and commodities as far back as he could, in some cases for up to 700 years when the information was available. Unfortunately, his published works are highly abstruse and difficult to read, as his theories are extensively punctuated with quotations from the Bible. Indeed, he made a point of not publishing his famous 'method'. In order to develop his ideas, he immersed himself in ancient mathematical teachings, particularly the works of Euclid, Pythagoras and Aristotle, as well as Eastern philosophy, astronomy and, of course, astrology. Gann was an avid astrologer, and it is reported that above his desk hung the astrological charts for the New York Stock Exchange, the US national chart and the Great Mutation conjunction of 1842, which many historians and astrologers have linked with the development of capitalism in the modern age. He was also a student of numerology and frequently claimed that his work was based on 'natural laws'. According to Gann, these laws gave the market a 'natural pace of movement', which followed certain trend lines that could be calculated.

Gann's methodology may have been eccentric and arcane, but his track record as a forecaster was impeccable. He accurately predicted the outbreak of war in 1914 and the subsequent stock market panic, as well as the armistice in 1918 and the abdication of the Kaiser. With uncanny precision, he foresaw the sequence of booms and panics of the 1920s, and was the only financial forecaster of note to foretell the Wall Street Crash of 1929, being the first to coin the phrase 'Black Friday'.

Gann devoted considerable time and energy to researching cycles, in particular the 10-year cycle in stock market averages that could clearly be observed to be operating over the 50-year period from 1873 to 1923. Although Dow and others had already noted the cycle, they had dismissed it out of hand as a mere curiosity and did not attempt to see whether it could be applied as a forecasting tool. Gann, however, felt that time (and by implication, cycles) is the most important factor influencing market movements, because the future always imitates the past, and each particular market is always working out time in relation to a previous time cycle. Gann distinguished two different kinds of time cycle – major cycles, which ranged from 90 down to 20 years, and minor cycles, which included the 10-year cycle he had already identified. In order to forecast the market accurately, Gann felt it was most important to know when the major cycles were due to turn, as the maximum amount of money could be made at the time of the greatest fluctuations in price.

Gann's 10-year cycle had already been noticed several years earlier by another researcher working on the other side of the Atlantic called Krohn, who in 1912 published one of the earliest extant astrological studies on the UK stock market and business cycle. In an article entitled 'Market Fluctuations and Business Crises in the Light of Astrology',[15] he noted that there exist both long-term and short-term modulations in economic activity. Krohn suggested that the long-term fluctuations related to the Jupiter–Saturn and Jupiter–Uranus cycles, with the conjunction and opposition points marking periods of 'crisis', by which he meant the beginning of a fall. As already noted, Jupiter and Saturn had already begun to be associated with business; Krohn followed this idea through to conclude that the cycle of these two planets must affect the level of business activity. His hypothesis is also a logical one when considered in astrological terms. Traditionally, Jupiter tends to expand whatever it influences and is therefore said to be favourable or 'benefic', whereas Saturn has the reverse effect of restricting and contracting, and often ushers in a time of scarcity and lack. Uranus, the third planet discussed by Krohn, is associated with sudden upsets, and unexpected, radical change. Consequently, when applied to the economy, the action of Uranus brings about sudden moves and changes.

Krohn ascribed the shorter-term fluctuations in the economy to the interaction between Jupiter, Saturn, Uranus and the planet Mars, i.e., the Mars–Jupiter, Mars–Saturn and Mars–Uranus cycles. The conjunction and opposition points were said to mark minimum prices, squares where prices peaked and trines to give a temporary rise which then died down again.

Krohn's study broke new ground because it was one of the first to take note of these important links between the economic and planetary cycles, and provided the theoretical foundation for much of the later work by other astrologers. His work is also noteworthy because he accurately identified the particular planets and cycles which later researchers confirmed as central to forecasting the behaviour of both the economy and the markets. It is a frequently observed quirk of scientific discovery that researchers working independently in the same field frequently arrive at the same conclusions at the same time. The significance of Krohn's findings is confirmed by the fact that just as he was publishing his results, another English astrologer, W. Gorn Old, writing under the pseudonym Sepharial, published *The Law of Values*,[16] in which he independently reached much the same conclusions as Krohn.

Krohn's study is also interesting as it embodies a key assumption made by virtually all the early analysts and researchers, but which certainly does not apply today. The fluctuations in the economy – the 'business crises' which Krohn took as his subject and which feature in the title of his study – and the movements of the stock market – 'market fluctuations' – are treated by Krohn as one and the same thing. This highlights the important point that in earlier times when the stock market was comparatively simple, it tended to mirror the ups and downs of the economy far more closely than it does today. At the time when Krohn was writing, for instance, an economic 'crisis' or recession would always cause a market fall; conversely, years in which there was steady growth in the economy would produce rising stock market prices as a matter of course.

Today, the relationship between the economy and stock market is far more complex and this means that the analysis of the early financial astrologers must be treated with caution. The essential difference lies in the fact that stock markets today are far more future-oriented and operate largely by discounting the future earnings of companies. The armies of analysts employed by stockbrokers are employed in trying to predict what these earnings will be two, three and even four years from today. So whilst the economy may be languishing in the depths of recession, the market will be looking to the recovery and will be rising at the same time as the economy at large is sliding further into recession. This produces the paradoxical situation where the stock market can be hitting new highs against a backdrop of unmitigated economic gloom! Today's cycles analysts must, at the very least, be careful to clearly differentiate economic cycles from market cycles, and should also make themselves aware of possible changes in economic relationships that have taken place over the last hundred years.

Fascinating though the early work might be, it is important to remember that correlations noted between planetary aspects or cycles and the economy or the markets a century ago may not work today, and readers should be wary of astrological studies based solely on early sources. If one is working with data covering a long period, a useful rule of thumb is to split the sample into two sections and see if a cycle derived from data for 1900–45, say, when the world's economies had a radically different structure from today, is still apparent in the data from 1945 to the present.

Another important point to bear in mind is that a cycle found in one country's economy or stock market is generally only relevant to that particular country or market. It is worth noting that few of the early researchers were cognisant of this factor and so virtually none of the early astrological studies discussed in this chapter take account of national differences. In research of this kind, it is also important to remain aware that different economies and stock markets do not always move in the same way at the same time, and different markets (bonds, currencies, stock markets, commodity markets, etc.) will all display their own distinct cycles. For example at the time of writing (1993), the US economy has shown clear signs of recovery, whilst at the same time all the economic reports from Germany indicate that there the recession is just beginning. As any market-watcher who works in an international context knows, the markets in different countries hit peaks and troughs at different times. Specific country-by-country market analysis will be discussed in greater detail in Chapters 4 and 5.

FINANCIAL ASTROLOGY IN THE 1930S

Just as in the preceding century, when the rapid expansion of speculation in the joint-stock companies had provided the impetus for sustained inquiry into the business cycle, so the generally depressed economic climate of the 1930s was the catalyst that sparked a new wave of interest in forecasting. And owing perhaps to the consistent failure of mainstream analysts to predict the Wall Street Crash of October 1929 and the decade of gloom that followed it, it was around this time that financial astrology, with its different perspective, began to really come into its own.

In the five-year period leading up to the Wall Street Crash, the United States of America enjoyed an unprecedented economic boom, as world trade had by then recovered sufficiently from the social and economic impact of the 1914–18 war to usher in a new round of industrial development and enterprise. Fuelled by dreams of instant wealth, many Americans threw themselves headlong into the speculative maelstrom, frequently financing their investments with borrowed funds secured by as little as a 10 per cent cash deposit. As prices on the New York Stock Exchange rose higher and higher, few stopped to ask when, if at all, the music might stop. And not a single financial analyst, with the exception of W. D. Gann, pinpointed October 1929 as the month when the biggest party in history would suddenly come to an abrupt end. It is hardly surprising, therefore, that the sober years that followed the Crash saw many more market-watchers take heed of what financial astrologers had to say. There was also a corresponding rise in the amount of research undertaken during these years, particularly in connection with the stock market, as astrologers worked patiently behind the scenes to refine and substantiate the growing body of forecasting knowledge.

One further development that enhanced the efficacy and power of financial astrology during this period was the discovery of the planet Pluto in 1930. When one considers the scene of economic chaos and disarray against which this discovery was made, it seems entirely appropriate that the action of Pluto is said to break down, destroy and transform whatever sphere of human activity and endeavour – be it the general economy or the stock market – it happens to be affecting at a given time. Pluto's discovery presented financial astrologers with new information, as well as the challenge of integrating its effects into their work. As we shall see, its presence also helped to explain various economic scenarios which had, up until this point, seemed difficult to fathom.

Against the backdrop of unrelenting economic contraction, deflation and gloom that epitomised the 1930s, two researchers, Langham working in the USA and Brahy working in Belgium, further developed some of the earlier astrological theories to produce more detailed analyses which not just described but quantified the effect of the planetary aspects for both the business cycle and the stock markets.

The American researcher Langham reached similar conclusions to the earlier workers, but provided some interesting numerical results that graphically illustrated how the aspects operated.[17,18] Using the Dow-Jones index for 1897–1932, he analysed the effect of 'good' aspects as compared to 'bad' aspects for the three planetary pairs Jupiter–Saturn, Jupiter–Uranus and Saturn–Uranus, using a 2-degree orb. He found the net Dow move in points to be:

	Number of occurrences	Rise in pts	Decline in pts	Net move
Saturn–Uranus	Good 11	46	24	+22
	Bad 19	21	140	119

		Number of occurrences	Rise in pts	Decline in pts	Net move
Jupiter–Uranus	Good	26	159	10	+149
	Bad	14	28	57	29
Jupiter–Saturn	Good	12	48	24	+24
	Bad	18	33	29	+4

	Good Aspects	Bad Aspects
Saturn–Uranus	30 60 120	45 90 135 180
Jupiter–Uranus	0 60 120	90 180
Jupiter–Saturn	60 120	45 90 180

In his discussion of these major planetary aspects, Langham says:

These planetary conditions foreshadow the rise and fall of general business conditions and commodity prices, and are a better index of production and trade than actual stock market prices, but the latter being largely dependent on trade conditions, follow the planetary indications closely.

Unfortunately, the correlations between stock market behaviour and planetary aspects noted by Langham no longer appear to work. A recent attempt to replicate his findings in today's stock markets did not prove successful. As already noted, economies and the stock market change their nature over time, and research soon becomes outmoded. Happily, some aspects of Langham's research have stood the test of time. When applied to the general economy, rather than the markets, his results are still valid, for the economy still appears to respond to the planetary aspects in the same way that it did in the 1930s. Indeed, Langham was right to say that the aspects he investigated are 'a better index of production and trade than actual stock market prices'.

Langham also noticed that the transits of Saturn and Uranus through the sign of Gemini tended to depress the USA's economy. Transits of Jupiter through Gemini, on the other hand, as would be expected from the planet of expansion, tended to increase economic activity. He also looked at the effects these planetary transits produced when referred to individual company charts, a topic we will return to in Chapter 6.

Meanwhile, the Belgian researcher Brahy went one step further than Langham in attempting to arrive at a quantitative evaluation of the relative effect of the various planetary aspects. In 1932,[19] he used 100 years of US stock market data and the aspects between Jupiter, Saturn, Uranus and Neptune to develop a weighting scheme, with the orbs and weights depending on the aspects. Brahy's work showed that the conjunction, opposition and trine had the widest orb, and the highest weight, and the semisquare and semisextile had the lowest.

Although Brahy did not provide any statistical analysis that showed how well his scheme would fare in practice, his work was important, as it introduced the idea of using a quantified model to make market predictions directly from the various planetary aspects. His work also illustrated yet another problem facing market-watchers wishing to utilise the early methods for making market predictions based on the various planetary aspects: namely, that there is frequently more than one aspect active at the same time. The unavoidable question soon arises: how much importance should be afforded to each aspect, and which planets act most strongly to determine the basic direction of the market? By developing the concept of a weighting system, Brahy's work went some way towards resolving this problem, and his approach was further refined and developed by the post-war researcher Donald Bradley (see below).[20]

Assessing the influence of the planets Jupiter, Saturn and Uranus was also a theme of the work of another Thirties researcher, L. J. Jensen, whose work, though little known, contains a number of important ideas.[21] Although he also evaluated the aspects of these three planets, and his analysis yielded the conclusion that Jupiter, Saturn and Uranus were significant as general economic indicators, they could not be relied upon to pinpoint the actual timing of either the economy or the stock market. To arrive at accurate forecasts, Jensen claimed it was necessary to look for a short-term 'trigger' as well as the longer-term aspects. Jensen was one of the first researchers to cast the transits of the faster-moving planets, such as Mercury or Mars, in this 'trigger' role, and thus further widened the spread of planetary factors that should be taken into consideration by financial forecasters. Interestingly, Jensen claimed that it was not only the traditional aspects, such as squares, conjunctions or oppositions, that could cause economic movements, but also lesser used aspects, such as the quintile (72 degrees, or one-fifth of the circle). In his fascinating analyses of the US national chart and the stock market chart, Jensen introduced the notion of how different countries will have different economic timings under the same planetary aspects because of their differing national natal charts, a factor rarely taken into account by other, more simplistic theories.

One of the first coherent attempts to create a complete astrological model of the business cycle, stock markets and individual companies was made by the American astrologer Louise McWhirter, who published her theory in 1938.[22] Taking as her starting-point the business cycle in the USA, she claimed that the main significator of the US economy was the backward movement of the Moon's Node through the astrological signs – a claim that we agree with and substantiate in the following chapter. The high point of business activity, according to McWhirter, occurs when the Node is in Leo. As the Node moves backward into Cancer and Gemini, activity starts falling. As the Node moves into Taurus, there is a transition to below average activity, which continues through to Aries and Pisces. The nadir of the cycle occurs when the Node is in the sign of Aquarius, and from here, as the Node moves on through Capricorn and Sagittarius, economic activity is still low, but rising – growth is positive. The transition to above average overall activity takes place in Scorpio. The final phase, with the Node in Libra and Virgo, has activity above average, and still rising back to the high point in Leo.

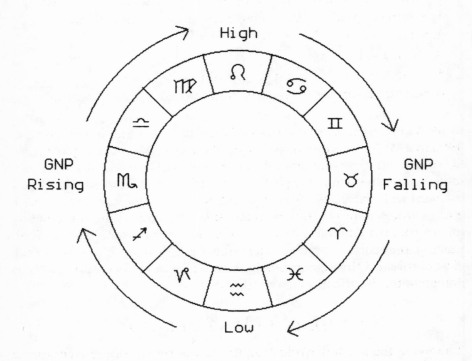

FIGURE 2.1: THE MCWHIRTER NODE CYCLE

McWhirter claimed that this basic cycle is modified by the effects of various secondary planetary factors. In particular, she noted that the following factors tended to increase economic activity:

1. Jupiter conjunct the Node.
2. Saturn trine, sextile or semisextile Uranus.
3. Jupiter in the signs of Gemini or Cancer.
4. Jupiter conjunct, sextile or trine Saturn or Uranus, but only when Saturn and Uranus are in aspect.
5. The Node in Gemini (a deviation from the basic Node cycle).
6. Trines or sextiles from the outer planets to Pluto.

Conversely, she claimed that the following factors tended to decrease activity:

1. Saturn conjunct, square or opposition the Node.
2. Saturn conjunct, square, semisquare or opposition Uranus.
3. Saturn in Gemini.
4. Uranus in Gemini.
5. Uranus conjunct, square or opposition the Node.
6. Square or opposition aspects from the outer planets to Pluto.

McWhirter's theory of the Moon's Node cycle was highly accurate and effective. As her theory can still be applied to the US economy of today, it has proved to be one of the few earlier models to have stood the test of time. For forecasting the performance of individual stocks, McWhirter worked with transits to the incorporation chart of the company, basing her interpretations on conventional astrology. The action of the newly discovered planet Pluto proved to be a highly significant factor in forecasting, particularly for the stock market, and McWhirter was one of the first astrologers to judge its business and financial effects correctly, and integrate this information into her model.

THE POST-WAR PERIOD

Following the Second World War, the development of early computer technology and more sophisticated methods of statistical analysis meant that more detailed research could be undertaken by analysts engaged in evaluating the cycles of the economy and the markets. Much of the research carried out in the 1950s took the work of earlier theorists as a starting-point and adapted and expanded it to reflect the increasingly complex structure of the Western economies.

Donald Bradley produced a forecasting theory that included the first fully quantified mathematical model of its kind and was in essence an attempt to produce a formula that combined the various planetary aspects. Bradley's work was an early prototype of the kind of methodology that is used in contemporary financial astrology, for he was one of the first researchers to combine many different cycles and aspects together to form a composite picture of future economic events. He noted that the 40-month business cycle (the Kitchin cycle) correlates with the con-junctions, squares and oppositions of the Jupiter–Uranus cycle, as these aspects occur on average 3.45 years apart. His model of the US stock market is noteworthy, in that it takes account of all the planets from Mercury to Pluto. As well as weighting the various aspects and planets, he introduced the declination cycles of Venus and Mars. For the purposes of forecasting, Bradley found the aspects of trine and sextile indicated a rising market, and square or opposition indicated a falling one; the conjunction, he found, could indicate either rises or falls, depending on the planets involved.

As the twentieth century wore on, astrologers gradually began to adopt a more cycles-based approach to the challenge of forecasting future events. The cyclical approach of the humanistic astrologers Dane Rudhyar and Alexander Ruperti was soon reflected in the work of financial astrologers like America's David Williams, who died in February 1993, and whose work since the 1950s constitutes one of the most important contributions to this field of research. Born in 1897, Williams was an engineer by train-ing and rose to the rank of Lieutenant Commander in the US Navy. In his spare time, however, he was a keen and experienced explorer of the common ground that lay between the planetary cycles of astrology and the cycles of business and finance. A frequent contributor to *Cycles* magazine, he also wrote extensively on such wide-ranging topics as astrology, business and stock market cycles, and mass psychology.

Williams is best known, however, for his work on the effects of mul-tiple aspects, which is explored in depth in his books, *Astro-Economics* (1959)[23] and *Financial Astrology* (1982).[24] To give an example: an oppo-sition of Saturn and Uranus would normally be expected to depress the economy, but if Jupiter, say, was trining Saturn at the same time, the effect of the unfavourable aspect between Saturn and Uranus would be neutralised. Williams provides several interesting examples of this kind of effect, and also discovered the seemingly paradoxical effect that, while the action of a sextile aspect is beneficial, the simultaneous occurrence of multiple sextiles tended to exert a downward, depressing influence.

In the 1970s too, the work of the Canadian astrologer Thomas Rieder foreshadowed some of the concepts now being developed by present-day financial astrologers. In *Astrological Warnings and the Stock Market* (1972),[25] Rieder highlights the significance for the stock market of the retrograde stations of Mars, which tend to produce a fall – but only when there is an outer planet in square or opposition to it and no alleviating trine or sextile from an outer planet at the same time. Rieder carried out extensive research into the US stock market and found that although this is not an infallible indicator – since not all such occurrences produce a fall – on those occasions when a fall does take place, the timing almost exactly corresponds to the date of the retrograde station.

Rieder also noted a four-and-a-half-year cycle in the Dow-Jones Index that could be linked to the Sun–Mars double (or sub-harmonic) cycle, making every alternate Mars retrograde station particularly powerful. His work on multiple cycles also finds parallels with some of the more advanced research being conducted at the present time. Finally, Rieder demonstrated an interesting method of short-term timing in the market using aspects of Mars and a tally of the Moon's aspects to indicate periods when the Moon is making mainly squares and oppositions (bearish) or mainly trines (bullish).

The phenomenon of 'triggering', whereby slow-moving cycles or aspects are activated into producing economic effects by faster-moving cycles or 'triggers', was also discussed around this time in the work of the American cycles researcher C. C. Matlock. He also developed a number of other important concepts relating to the influence of the planets and the solar system on the economy and the stock markets in his book *Man and Cosmos* (1977).[26]

In the late 1970s and early 1980s, financial astrology took a great leap forward as a result of the new developments in information technology that took place at that time. When personal computers began to find their way into the world's offices, homes and financial organisations for the first time, financial astrology suddenly entered a new era. Up to this point, researchers and astrologers had been held back by the sheer impracticability of the number of calculations required to produce accurate financial forecasts. Now it became possible to perform these detailed procedures in minutes or seconds, rather than days or even weeks.

The bespoke astrological computer programs produced by Robert Hand and Michael Erlewine catapulted financial astrology far beyond the previous limitations that had restricted its scope of influence, and ushered in a new universe of possibilities. These new possibilities are still unfolding and evolving, as new programs and techniques are developed year by year.

To begin our exploration of financial astrology, however, we should return to the point at which we began, and turn our attention to the same questions that preoccupied Herschel's learned intellect all those decades ago: What is the cause of the business cycle? And how can it be predicted?

Financial astrology, as we shall see, is uniquely fitted to answer those questions.

References

1. Herschel W., *Philosophical Transactions*, Royal Society of London, 1801.
2. Jevons, W. S., 'The Solar Period and the Price of Corn', British Association for the Advancement of Science, 1875.
3. Garcia-Mata C. and Shaffner, F. I., 'Solar and Economic Relationships', *Quarterly Journal of Economics*, Vol. 49, 1934.
4. Carrington, R. C., *Observations of the Spots on the Sun*, Williams & Norgate, London, 1863.
5. Norton, W. A., *A Treatise on Astronomy*, John Wiley & Sons Inc., New York, 1867.
6. De La Rue, Stewart and Loewy, 'Researches on Solar Physics', *Proceedings*, Royal Society of London, Vol. 18, 1869–70. See also: 'Investigations of Planetary Influences', *Proceedings*, Royal Society of London, Vol. 20, 1871–2.
7. Brown, E. W., 'A Possible Explanation of the Sunspot Period', *Monthly Notices*, Royal Astronomical Society, Vol. 60, Number 10, London, 1900.
8. Bollinger, C. J., *Atlas of Planetary and Solar Climate*, Battenberg Press, 1960 edition.
9. Wood, K. D., 'Sunspots and Planets', *Nature*, Vol. 240, 10 November, 1972.
10. Clark, H., *The Railway Magazine and Annals of Science*, ed. J. Herapath, 1838.
11. Clark, H. ed., *Railway Register*, 1847.
12. Kitchen, J., *Review of Econonic Statistics*, Harvard University Press, Vol. 5, January 1923.
13. Beveridge, W. H., 'Weather and Harvest Cycles', *Economic Journal*, Vol. 31, 1921, pp.429–52.
14. Beveridge, W. H., 'Wheat Prices and Rainfall in Western Europe', *Journal*, Royal Statistical Society, Vol. 85, 1922, pp.412–59.
15. Krohn, L., 'Market Fluctuations and Business Crises in the Light of Astrology', *Modern Astrology*, Vol. IX, 1912, pp.451–56.
16. Sepharial (pseud. of W. Gorn Old), *The Law of Values*, London, 1913.
17. Langham, J. M., *Planetary Effects on Stock Market Prices*, Maghal, Los Angeles, 1932.

18. Langham, J. M., *Cyclical Market Forecasting Stocks and Grain*, Maghal, Los Angeles, 1938.

19. Brahy, G. L., *La Clef de la Prévision des Evénements Mondiaux et des Fluctuations Economiques et Boursières*, Editions PIC, Brussels, 3rd edition, 1968.

20. Bradley, D. A., *Stock Market Prediction*, Llewellyn, 1950 and 1968.

21. Jensen, L. J., *Astro-Cycles and Speculative Markets*, Lambert-Gann, 1978 edition (originally 1935, 38 and 61).

22. McWhirter, L., *The McWhirter Theory of Stock Market Forecasting*, Astro Book Co., New York, 1938.

23. Williams, D., *Astro-Economics*, Llewellyn, 1959.

24. Williams, D., *Financial Astrology*, American Federation of Astrologers, 1982.

25. Rieder, T., *Astrological Warnings and the Stock Market*, Pagurian Press, Toronto, 1972.

26. Matlock, C. C., *Man and Cosmos*, Development Cycles Research Project, Waynesville, NC, USA, 1977.

3

Predicting the Economy

As the major economies of the Western world emerge, battle-scarred, from the worst recession since the Second World War, three further questions will undoubtedly be uppermost in the minds of all those involved in business and financial forecasting. The first question is surely: Why didn't anyone see the recession coming? But, since recrimination is a luxury that most businesses can ill afford, the second and far more pressing question must be: How will we know when recovery has really begun and it's safe to believe what the politicians say? And finally: How will we know when growth has peaked and another recession is about to start?

Happily, the cycles-based analysis of financial astrology provides a well-proven conceptual framework within which all these questions, and many others besides, can be satisfactorily answered. Using the insights afforded by planetary cycles, several British astrologers were able to detect the 1990s recession well in advance, a predictive success than none of their more orthodox colleagues in the forecasting field were able to match. Lest this be dismissed as a fortuitous fluke or 'flash in the pan', readers should remember that financial astrology has consistently produced systematic and accurate forecasts over the decades. Using the same cyclical techniques employed by today's astrologers, W. D. Gann successfully predicted the onset of the Great Depression in the 1930s, at a time when the US economy was still basking in prosperity, and the erstwhile experts of the Harvard Economic Society were proclaiming that an end to growth was unthinkable.

Thanks to the technological revolution that has transformed financial astrology, there is no mystique attached to these impressive forecasts. No occult skills are required in order to produce similar results – merely the application and elbow grease needed to sit before a computer and sift through many years of data and information! Experience has shown that the rise and fall of business and financial cycles correlates well with planetary cycles and can be predicted with ease once the basic principles of this cyclical approach have been fully understood.

The main thrust of the research carried out by financial astrologers over the last century or so has been towards identifying the main planetary cycles which affect the business cycle, the alternating periods of growth and recession in the economy. The early researchers correctly saw that the most powerful cycles to affect the economy are the longer-term ones formed by the interaction of the five outer planets – Jupiter, Saturn, Uranus, Neptune and Pluto – and it is these cycles which form a major focus of discussion in this chapter.

Predicting the economy, however, is not simply a matter of cycles. As our aim in these pages is to produce a comprehensive model of the economy which can provide a basis for predictions and forecasts, we need to look at the whole picture. This means introducing some additional factors, namely planetary aspects and national charts.

The early researchers concentrated on the aspects between the outer planets and had *some* success correlating these with economic turning-points. More recent work has shown that the whole cycle between two planets is important – economic change does not occur in jumps at the time of planetary aspects, but is a continuous process. It should not be assumed, however, that aspects are unimportant. The aspects formed by the faster-moving planets, such as Mars, can act as triggers for the slower-moving outer planet cycles. In addition, when a major aspect between two outer planets links into the national chart for a particular country, then that aspect will be particularly emphasised in that country and the economy more strongly influenced there than elsewhere.

The national chart serves to bring the aspects down to earth and shows which countries will respond to their influence most strongly. The chart factor also helps to explain why the UK, USA and Germany, for example, have in recent years all experienced varying degrees of recession at slightly different times, as the planetary configurations link (or fail to link) into each country's chart.

To begin creating an astrological model of the economy, however, we must first turn our attention to cycles.

PLANETARY CYCLES AND THE ECONOMY

The use of planetary cycles for financial forecasting has a long history. As far back as 1543, Christopher Kurz of Antwerp devised an astrological system for predicting the money market which met with modest success. In 1876, Samuel Brenner of Cleveland, Ohio, used the Jupiter cycle as the basis for a set of predictions published in *Brenner's Prophecies of Future Ups and Downs in Prices* and, happily, these forecasts also proved to be reasonably accurate. Essentially, however, the development of cycles as a predictive tool in the financial sector is a comparatively recent phenomenon, since the complex procedure of using multiple cycles to arrive at an accurate 'print-out' of the nation's economy has developed as a direct result of the computer revolution that transformed the entire financial sector in the 1980s.

So how do these planetary cycles actually work? Cycles are a dynamic way of interpreting the relationship between two planets moving at different speeds and a complete cycle can be measured as the period between two successive conjunctions of these two planets. Between conjunctions, the planets will move through the entire sequence of aspects – sextile, square, trine, opposition and back to conjunction. Using planetary cycles gives us the opportunity to work with the unfolding pattern of astrological events, in addition to the fixed series provided by the aspects. This is a great advantage for, as we will see, economic events do not always correspond directly to aspect patterns and it is only by taking a cyclical approach that we can begin to understand what is happening in the economy. The sequence of diagrams accompanying this chapter shows how the unfolding cycles of the outer planets relate to the cycle of the economy.

Planetary cycles correspond to the underlying structure or 'backbone' of the economy and are fundamental to understanding medium and long-term economic trends. Forecasting the economy involves working with the slower-moving cycles based on the movements of the outer planets. The shorter cycles of Mercury, Venus and Mars, although more widely used in stock market forecasting, also have a role to play here, for they often fill in important details in the overall picture and can also trigger the long-term cycles into manifestation. Identifying the cycles that affect each country's economy and assessing how they operate together allows us to produce a forecast of what will happen if the cycles continue to affect economic growth as they have done in the past. This is the basis on which the predictions in this chapter have been made.

Predicting the economy involves considering the simultaneous interaction of many different cycles and charts, and one should never make the mistake of looking for an isolated 'cause' for any economic turning-point. As always in financial astrology, it is vital to look at the overall picture. Clearly, no single cycle can be picked out as the 'cause' of economic growth and recession. If this were the case, that cycle would have been identified long ago and astrological forecasting would be a very simple process – but also a rather boring one. Indeed, it is the very fact that there are so many cycles at work, sometimes reinforcing each other, sometimes cancelling each other out, that makes the astrological analysis of the economy (and the stock market) such an interesting process.

The major outer planet cycles provide vital information not only about growth and recession, but also about other economic variables, such as inflation. Not only do different cycles affect different countries but also different economic variables within each country. For instance, the Moon's Node cycle tells us a great deal about economic growth in the US, but not about inflation.

In addition to the Moon's Node cycle, there are nine outer planet cycles based on the relationship between the five outer planets. The periods of their heliocentric cycles are as follows (in years):

Jupiter–Saturn:	19.86
Jupiter–Uranus:	13.81
Jupiter–Neptune:	12.78
Jupiter–Pluto:	12.46
Saturn–Uranus:	45.36
Saturn–Neptune:	35.87
Saturn–Pluto:	33.46
Uranus–Neptune:	171.38
Uranus–Pluto:	127.48
Moon's Node:	18.6

These cycles have been linked with various facets of business and commerce; all have different roles to play in shaping economic activity and each has a distinctly different economic 'theme'. For example, financial astrologers have found that the 45-year Saturn–Uranus cycle, one of the main cycles used for analysing the UK economy, is an important determinant of investment and production in heavy industry, as the peaks and troughs in the investment cycle correlate closely with those of the planetary cycle.

By contrast, the Saturn–Pluto cycle is often linked with the need to get back to basics and purge the basic structures of the economy. The Saturn–Pluto cycle is also an important indicator of stock market trends, as we shall see in Chapters 4 and 5.

The Jupiter–Uranus cycle is closely linked to the free market economies, and is one of the key cycles operating in both the UK and US economies. The research of the American astrologer David Williams has graphically shown how powerful the effects of this cycle can be. He wrote, 'Since 1762, the beginning of each new cycle [the conjunction] has, with only two exceptions, coincided with low periods of business activity in the US.' These include the recessions of 1803, 1844, 1900, 1914, 1927 and 1941 – to name but a few. This cycle was also a contributing factor in the Great Depression of the 1930s.

The Jupiter–Pluto cycle – another 'free market' cycle – is also strongly connected with the Western economies, particularly the UK and the US, and is linked with issues of financial and political power.

The Uranus–Neptune cycle is yet another major long-term cycle which affects the Western industrialised nations and it is linked to the interplay of capital (Uranus) and labour (Neptune). As the cycle moves so slowly, it does not correlate with short-term market moves, or even with longer economic cycles, but rather indicates the unfolding of the broad social and economic changes that take place over many decades.

The Uranus–Neptune cycle has been of particular interest recently, as 1993 saw a conjunction of these two planets, an event which takes only once in every 172 years. Predicting the likely effects of the conjunction presented a problem, however, because no detailed records exist for economic activity in 1821, the year when this aspect last occurred, still less for 1650, when the previous conjunction occurred. Since the conjunction in 1821, however, the world has seen the rise of capitalism and the industrial economies, as well as the development of organised labour in the form of unions, and the rise and fall of the socialist states in Eastern Europe. The major aspect points have marked important times in the relationship between free enterprise and labour, and it is likely that the new cycle now beginning could well indicate a long-term move towards a post-industrial society.

WHY RECESSIONS HAPPEN: THE JUPITER–SATURN CYCLE

This cycle, which is about 20 years in length, is formed by the interaction of the two 'business planets': Jupiter, the planet of expansion, optimism and success, and Saturn, the planet of restriction, pessimism and contraction. The interplay between these two planetary energies correlates closely to the rhythms of growth and recession in the economy, and provides an important and surprisingly accurate guide to timing the broad sweep of economic activity.

Research has shown that the Jupiter–Saturn cycle is perhaps *the* most important cycle for predicting the economy. This claim is not based on theory, but on the practical evidence of history. Earlier this century, as the world economies collapsed into the slump years of the Great Depression, the Jupiter–Saturn cycle was found to have played a key role in the economic collapse. In the early 1990s too, the Jupiter–Saturn cycle was again reaching a crucial point just prior to the onset of recession. This was the main reason why financial astrologers were predicting the economic downturn which other forecasters so vehemently denied would take place. For on the basis of the evidence, the astrologers knew only too well that when the Jupiter–Saturn cycle is at a critical point, recession is seldom far away.

Long before the Second World War, the American W. D. Gann was one of the first analysts to perceive the relevance of the Jupiter–Saturn cycle to the business cycle, observing that almost exactly every 20 years there was a huge wave of speculation followed by a boom economy and in due course by huge losses. This 20-year cycle was played out in the speculative boom of the 1920s and was also uncannily mirrored by the boom years of the 1980s. Each time, Gann noted, the boom came to an end when a Jupiter–Saturn opposition took place: the series of oppositions and their resultant effects can be seen on the graphs (Figs. 3.1–3.3) in 1911, 1930 and 1951. The link between the Jupiter–Saturn cycle and the cycle of economic activity is too strong to be denied.

But more importantly, Gann discovered that this 20-year Jupiter–Saturn cycle was underpinned by a deeper cycle: a triple cycle of Jupiter and Saturn. He noticed that every 60 years, each third opposition in the Jupiter–Saturn cycle inevitably ushered in a major recession in all the leading world economies and he correctly identified this triple Jupiter–Saturn cycle as one of the main causes of the Great Depression.

The triple cycle of Jupiter and Saturn is so powerful in its effects because it marks the point when the two 'business planets' link together particularly strongly. Every 60 years, the difficult or 'hard' opposition of Jupiter to Saturn coincides with five complete cycles of Jupiter round the Sun (each about 12 years long) and two complete cycles of Saturn round the Sun (each about 30 years long). Gann named the triple cycle 'the master time cycle', an appropriate title given the power and scope of its influence on the global economy and its great significance as a financial forecasting tool.

The Jupiter–Saturn triple cycle provides the key to understanding just why the recession of the early 1990s has been so deep and long-lasting. The economic history of the past 200 years clearly shows that every 60 years, the triple Jupiter–Saturn cycle opposition is *always* immediately followed by a major world recession considerably more severe in its effects than the periodic downturns that occur in between these 60-year points. The best-known example of the triple cycle opposition aspect is

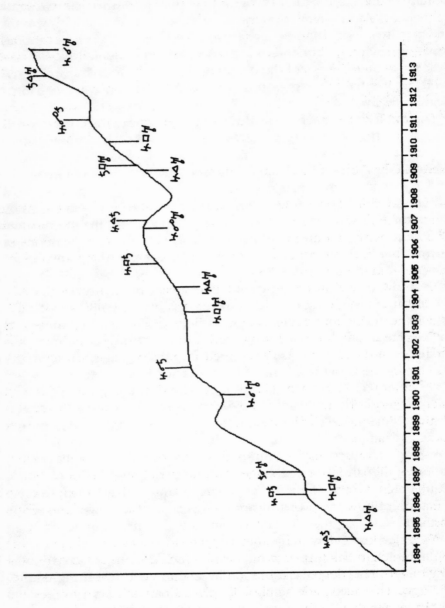

FIGURE 3.1: UK GNP AND ASPECTS, 1894–1914

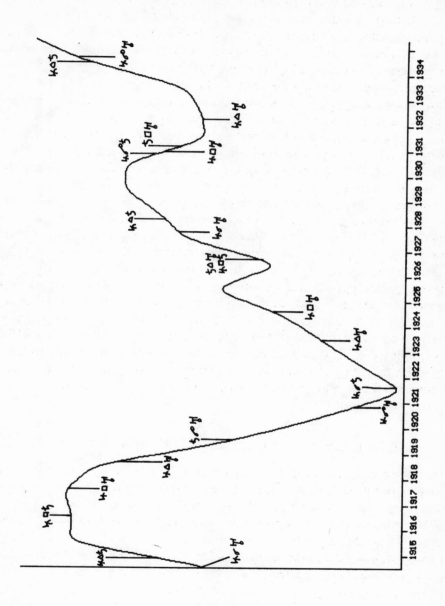

FIGURE 3.2: UK GNP AND ASPECTS, 1914–35

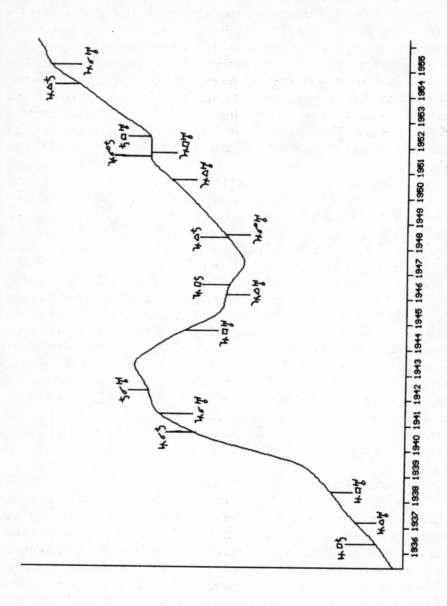

FIGURE 3.3: UK GNP AND ASPECTS, 1935–55

the Great Depression of the 1930s, when the US took 3½ years to hit bottom, and the economy shrank by a total of 30 per cent. Contrast this contraction with the relatively minor recession of 1981–2, when the US GNP shrank by a mere 2 per cent. In this case, the recession was not caused by the triple cycle and so its effects were markedly less severe. Looking back another 60 years, however, the opposition of 1871 also marked the start of another deep recession, from which the US economy did not fully recover for five long years. Moving 60 years back again, the triple cycle opposition in 1811 was the cue for yet another severe recession. The evidence of history is compelling. Every 60 years a major recession takes place and there have been no exceptions to this rule.

One of the main characteristics of these major recessions is an almost total loss of business confidence, which even the most strenuous economic palliatives of government fail to remedy. In the Great Depression, as in the 1990s, interest rates fell to record lows, touching 2 per cent at one point in the 1930s, but even this could not revive investment until the downturn had fully played itself out.

On this basis, if we look forward 60 years from the Great Depression of the 1930s to 1990, it seems almost gratuitous to point out that the recession which began in 1990 – the worst economic downturn for six decades – coincided yet again with a Jupiter–Saturn triple cycle opposition. Now we can begin to see why the world's financial astrologers were predicting in 1989 that a recession would begin the following year, at a time when many economists considered it unlikely. Knowing the past history of the cycle and the harshness of its effects, the astrological forecasters were confident in predicting that the recession of the 1990s would be unusually deep and long-lasting. Unlike the economists, who predicted at the onset of the recession that it would be short and shallow.

It is also interesting to speculate whether the Jupiter–Saturn triple cycle was in fact the 'long wave' that Kondratieff tentatively identified in 1926, when he announced his discovery of a 47–60 year cycle in US economic activity. All the evidence points to the fact that this was indeed so and that yet another independent researcher had alighted on this important cycle, whose effects we now know to be so profound and far-reaching.

There are other causes of recession which will be discussed in due course, but the Jupiter–Saturn triple cycle is a very reliable and important significator of economic decline. Fortunately, the triple cycle opposition is not due to take place again until 2050, so it will not constitute cause for concern in the near future!

The Jupiter–Saturn triple cycle is one of the key cycles involved in causing global recession. But in order to discover the underlying factors that cause the economy to turn at other times and in individual countries, such as the USA, we must now look at some other cycles.

THE MOON'S NORTH NODE CYCLE: THE KEY US CYCLE

One of the most important US cycles is that of the Moon's Node. Unlike the other cycles considered here, the Nodal cycle does not involve a cycle between two planets, but rather a cycle through the zodiac, a cycle which the 1930s astrologer Louise McWhirter found had a powerful and persistent correlation with the American economy. Her research showed that many recessions in the US can be explained and predicted by the cycle, and so it is an invaluable guide to US economic activity. We looked at this cycle briefly in Chapter 2. To show how it works, we will now examine the cycle in more detail.

Taking the period from 1889 to 1988, we note the change in GNP at each point in the 18.6 year Node cycle. By repeating this over each occurrence of the cycle in the data and averaging the result for each position of the Node, we get the graph shown in Fig. 3.4. (Note that unlike the other cycles we shall be looking at in this chapter, the Moon's Node moves *backwards* through the zodiac.) The Node cycle acts very strongly on the US economy, giving a swing of plus or minus 3½ per cent in annual growth over the cycle. This is a graph of GNP, not of annual change, so that when the graph is falling there is a contraction in the economy and when it rises the economy is growing.

McWhirter found that the low point of US economic activity is reached when the North Node transits through Aquarius. This shows up clearly in the graph where we see the economy falling through Pisces and reaching a nadir in Aquarius. From this point, GNP rises through Aquarius and Capricorn until we reach Sagittarius and Scorpio. Here, however, we find the main area of difference from McWhirter's results, because it can clearly be seen that the economy falls or is flat at this time. From Scorpio, there is a steady rise through Libra and Virgo until the economy reaches a peak in Leo, exactly as McWhirter suggested. When the Node enters Cancer, the economy begins to fall, again as she suggested. There is a slight rise in Gemini, one of the special exceptions to the Nodal cycle which McWhirter correctly identified. (See Chapter 2 for a full account of McWhirter's modifying factors.) From this point onwards, the economy begins to fall again before reaching its low point in Aquarius.

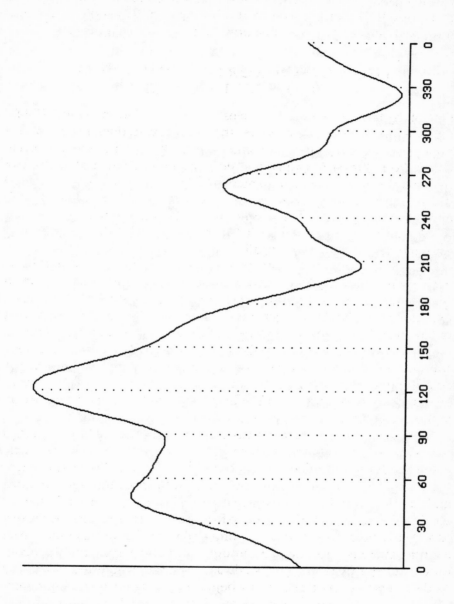

FIGURE 3.4: NODE CYCLE IN US GNP

McWhirter's work was first published in 1938 and it provides an aston-ishingly accurate cyclical guide to the pattern of the US economy in the post-war era. Using the Nodal cycle, the timing of recession can be accurately pinpointed not just once, but time and again. For instance, in 1969–71, the Node transited through Pisces and Aquarius, producing a recession, as McWhirter would have predicted. In 1989–90, the Node transited through Aquarius again, triggering the early 1990s recession and demonstrating once again the predictive power of this cycle for the US economy.

McWhirter also accurately identified several factors which modify the basic Node cycle and these are relevant to the time-scale of the 1990s recession. The recovery that might have been expected from her model once the Node had passed the low point in Aquarius was delayed for two reasons. Firstly, the Node made a conjunction with Saturn in early 1991 and then a conjunction with Uranus in late 1991. As McWhirter found that both these factors tended to depress economic activity, the delayed upturn is further proof of the validity of her findings. When applied to the US economy, therefore, the Nodal cycle works extremely well and is simple, elegant and impressively accurate.

But unlike the Jupiter–Saturn triple cycle, which operates globally, the Nodal cycle does not work well for other world economies. Looking at how the cycle works in the context of the UK economy, Fig. 3.5, a some-what different picture emerges. Although there are some similarities that can be observed – there is a rise in Capricorn and fall in Sagittarius and Scorpio, as well as a rise in Libra and Virgo – the overall pattern does not conform to the pattern which McWhirter identified for the US. It should also be noted that the amplitude of the cycle for the UK is plus or minus 1½ per cent in annual growth over the cycle, less than half that found for the US economy, showing that the Node's cycle has a much weaker effect on the UK economy than that of the US.

McWhirter's pioneering work has not only stood the test of time, but also clearly shows that the Moon's Node cycle is first and foremost a key cycle for predicting the US economy. The next peak in the Node cycle occurs in 1999 and the next low point in 2008–9.

Our original thesis – that different countries have their own individ-ual cycles – is now shown to be firmly grounded in economic reality, for the Nodal cycle shows us that the same planetary cycle will affect individual economies in a very different way. Although certain cycles, such as the Jupiter–Saturn cycle, act globally, other cycles influence some countries more strongly than others. And even if the overall shape of the cycle is similar, small variations in the position of turning-points in

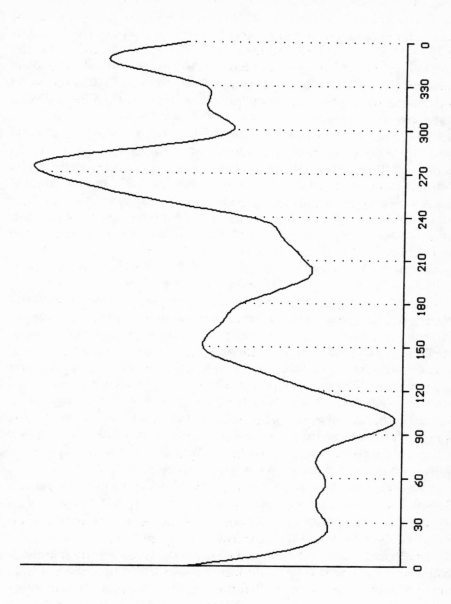

FIGURE 3.5: NODE CYCLE IN UK GNP

the cycle will cause important differences in the timing of recession and recovery from country to country.

PLANETARY CYCLES IN THE ECONOMY

Since each country has its own individual 'set' of cycles, one of the main objectives of financial astrologers has been to identify the particular cycles that act most strongly in each nation. Just as the Moon's Node cycle acts strongly on the US economy, so the UK too has its own set of cycles which can be used to predict the pattern of future growth. These include three cycles of Jupiter: the Jupiter–Saturn cycle, the Jupiter–Uranus cycle and the Jupiter–Pluto cycle, as well as the Saturn–Uranus cycle and a solar cycle. The Jupiter–Saturn cycle has already been discussed in some detail as a significator of recession. Now we will look at the Jupiter–Uranus cycle and Jupiter–Pluto cycle – which have important roles to play in both the UK and the US.

The Jupiter–Uranus Cycle

The 14-year Jupiter–Uranus cycle is a very important one for the capitalist and 'free-market' economies, and also functions as a measure of the state of the markets. The cycle works well as an indicator of economic activity in both the US and the UK, but there are interesting differences which can be observed by comparing the cycle graphs for the two countries. Taking the Jupiter–Uranus cycle as shown in Fig. 3.6, we can see how UK GNP changes over the cycle. We have a strong cycle with an amplitude of about plus/minus 2 per cent growth per year. Note that the fall stops at the opposition (180 degrees separation) but the other aspects are not strongly marked. We will return to this later.

The comparable graph for the Jupiter–Uranus cycle in the US, Fig. 3.7, shows a similar picture to the UK, but with some important differences. In both countries, there is a peak at 60 degrees separation and then a fall to just after the opposition at 180 degrees separation. The rise back to the peak, however, is different in the two countries. In the UK, the economy remains flat after the opposition aspect and starts to rise at 300 degrees (the incoming sextile). The rise continues through the conjunction (0 degrees) back to the peak at 60 degrees. In the US, however, there is a strong turn just after the opposition, with a very rapid rise until 240 degrees (the incoming trine). From here the US economy is relatively flat, with minor ups and downs until the final rise through the conjunction back to the 60-degree point.

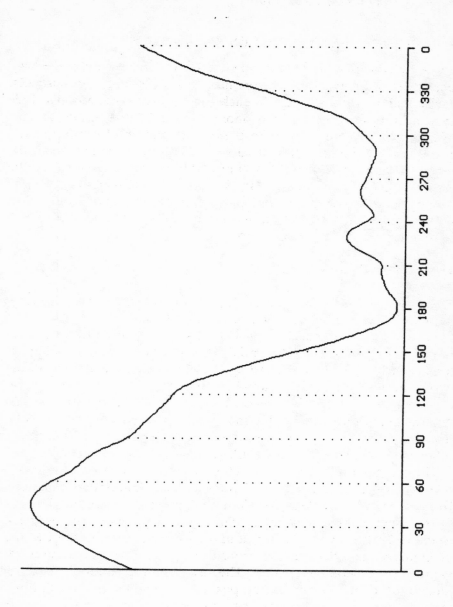

FIGURE 3.6: JUPITER–URANUS CYCLE IN UK GNP

Money and the Markets

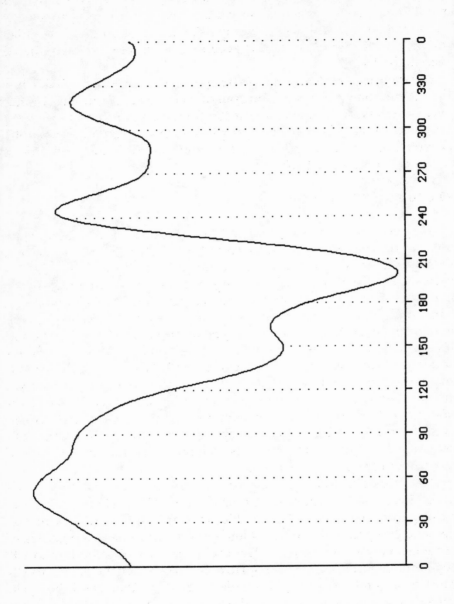

FIGURE 3.7: JUPITER–URANUS CYCLE IN US GNP

Although the overall pattern is similar in both economies, it is interesting to note that, according to this cycle, recovery from recession occurs at a different point in each country. Also recovery in the US appears to be much stronger, with the economy rising far more quickly and earlier than in the UK, although the rise occurs over a shorter period in the US than in the UK.

The cycle can be clearly seen to be operating at the end of 1980, when the UK economy was just coming out of recession as the Jupiter–Uranus cycle was making its final sextile at 300 degrees. Again, in October 1993, the cycle was at its final incoming sextile and this was therefore the point at which the UK economy started to come properly out of the deep recession of the early 1990s.

The Jupiter–Pluto Cycle

Turning now to the Jupiter–Pluto cycle for both countries, a different picture can be seen. Since the outermost planet Pluto was only discovered in 1930, little research of any significance on the effects of the planet's cycles was carried out until the 1940s. Since then research has shown that Pluto is very important in business forecasting, having a powerful effect on both the economy and stock market. Fig. 3.8 shows the economic effects of the Jupiter–Pluto cycle as applied to both the UK and US economies. The low point of the cycle is common to both countries and takes place just after the 60-degree sextile. The two countries also share the subsequent rise, which runs up to the opposition for the UK and just before the trine in the US. From this point, we can see falls for both the UK and the US, with a slight rise in the last 30 degrees of the cycle for the US. By the time the cycle reaches the conjunction, both economies are contracting, and this continues until the sextile point of 60 degrees of separation is reached.

The cycle helps to explain the very strong growth which took place in the UK in 1972 through to the first half of 1973, when Jupiter was moving from 70 degrees ahead of Pluto towards the first trine, which is the strongest part of the Jupiter–Pluto cycle's rising phase and generally produces very strong growth. The cycle also provides the key to UK economic patterns in 1983 through to early 1984, when the dip in growth came to an end just as Jupiter made a sextile to Pluto and the cycle entered a strong rising phase: as the cycle predicted, growth shot back up again in 1984.

The Jupiter–Pluto cycle thus operates *almost* identically in the UK and US. The Jupiter–Uranus cycle operates similarly in each country,

Money and the Markets

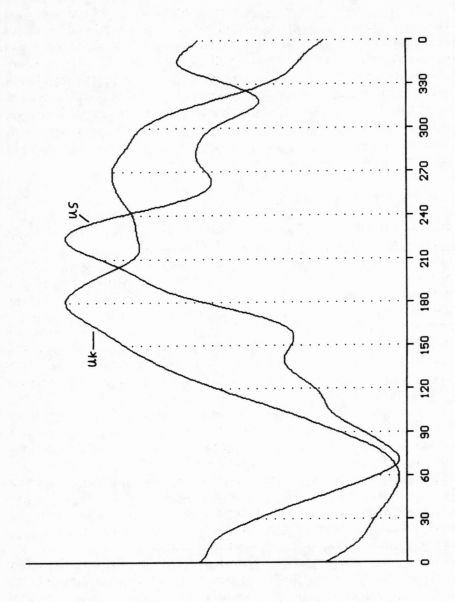

FIGURE 3.8: JUPITER–PLUTO CYCLE IN UK AND US GNP

but gives an important timing difference in the recovery from the low point of the cycle. These variations serve to illustrate once again how important it is to analyse each economy separately so as to gain an accurate impression of the effects of each cycle. The way planetary separations affect the UK will always differ from the way they affect the German economy and, as we see, the US will be different again. There are no short-cuts when it comes to astrological forecasting, for the simple reason that there are no planetary cycles that give identical results in all countries. Each country and its cycles must therefore *always* be treated as an individual case. The Jupiter–Saturn triple cycle is the closest we have to a universal cycle, but even here there are significant timing differences in each country.

PREDICTING THE UK ECONOMY

Looking once more at the UK economy and the predictions that can be made for the next few years, Fig. 3.9 illustrates the effects of the five major UK cycles – Jupiter–Saturn, Jupiter–Uranus, Jupiter–Pluto, Saturn–Uranus and the solar cycle – on the UK economy. If the cycles continue to operate as they have done over the last 150 years, we can combine the effect of each cycle into a model of the UK economy and arrive at the prediction shown in the graph. It should be noted that the data used to derive these cycles is from 1830 to 1988. The analysis was stopped at 1988 so that the prediction from 1988 would not be based on a period used to derive the model and could therefore be compared to the actual outcome.

Combining these cycles gives us a clear forecast of the recession of the early 1990 and also of the very long period during which growth remains negative. Whilst the cycles approach gives us only general indications about the state of the economy and should not be relied upon to provide exact, to the month, timing, the overall prediction nevertheless coincides very closely with the actual pattern of events. Although the predictive model and actual outcome do not always totally coincide during the period from which the model is derived, the major swings between growth and recession are clearly indicated.

The cycles model therefore provides us with a good overall picture of the economy. On this basis, it is possible to predict that 1993 will see recovery (growth above zero), but with a fall back to zero growth by the end of 1994. According to this model, only in 1995 and 1996 will we see the UK economy move back into solid and sustained growth. This is a general, cycles-based forecast. Later in this chapter we will explore

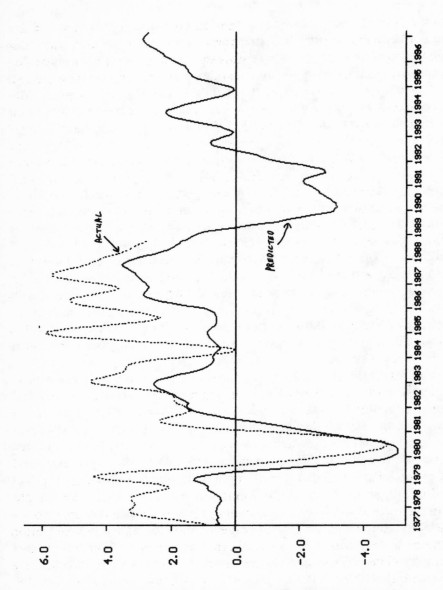

FIGURE 3.9: UK GNP ANNUAL PERCENTAGE CHANGE
– ACTUAL AND PREDICTED

the astrological aspects that are operating over the same period and these will enable us to fine-tune our predictions for economic recovery.

Forecasting UK Inflation

The cycles used in financial astrology also show a high degree of correlation with many other financial variables, such as inflation. Although inflation is often seen as a comparatively recent economic bugbear, history shows that periods of price stability have alternated with periods of quite high inflation on a number of occasions in the past. Occasionally, prices have been known to rise so rapidly that the currency has become worthless, as in the German hyper-inflation of 1922–3. In the UK, retail price inflation reached 12 per cent per year in 1951–2 and a staggering 25 per cent in 1975! Equally, the country has witnessed several periods of negative inflation, such as during 1922 and from 1929 to mid-1933 during the Great Depression when prices actually fell from year to year. The techniques of financial astrology make it possible to predict both the long-term and short-term cycles of inflation, an important advantage to those involved in business and investment planning.

As with UK GNP, not just one but several cycles are involved in producing the rise and fall of inflation, and a particularly important one is the Saturn–Neptune heliocentric cycle, shown in Fig. 3.10. Since this is one of the longer cycles (36 years), it is not useful as a marker of monthly changes in inflation, but provides a guide to the way periods of higher than average inflation alternate with those in which prices rise more slowly than average.

One of the most remarkable features of this cycle is its smoothness, which is clearly shown by the graph. There is no evidence of any effect at the traditional aspect points of the square (90 and 270 degrees) or the trine (at 120 and 240 degrees). It is a strong cycle, but again there are no clear aspect points. What stands out is a marked splitting into two parts (note that this is a graph of the price level with the trend removed, not of the inflation rate). From the conjunction to the opposition, prices tend to fall, so the rate of inflation is lower than average. Conversely, from the opposition back to the conjunction, prices tend to rise, so the rate of inflation is higher than average. Over the roughly 36-year period of the cycle, therefore, we have an alternation, whereby 18 years of below average inflation is followed by 18 years of above average inflation. We are currently (1993) in the below average inflation phase of this cycle.

As with all the other economic variables discussed in this book, such as the rate of growth or movements of the stock market, underlying the

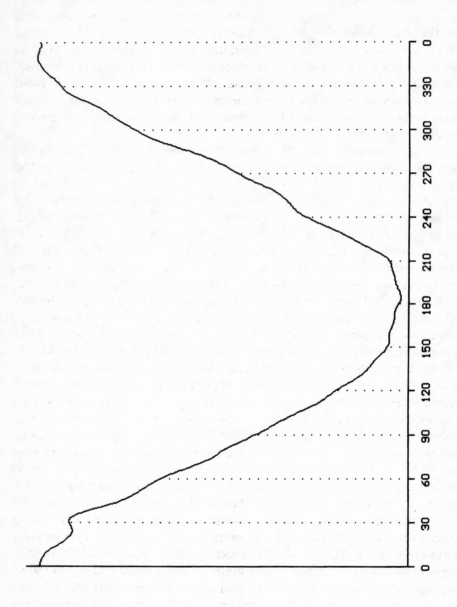

FIGURE 3.10: SATURN–NEPTUNE CYCLE IN UK INFLATION

yearly changes in inflation there are both long-term and short-term factors at work. The interaction of short-term cycles can produce quite strong moves even from relatively low amplitude cycles, as sometimes the different cycles will all come together and all rise or all fall at the same time. When the different influences all combine in this way, a strong move can result. Similarly, the interaction of long cycles of, say, 20- or 30-years' duration, can give rise to what appear to be short-term effects, purely from the way they sometimes reinforce or sometimes cancel out. It is the interaction of a number of different cycles that is important – not just one or two in isolation.

One of the shorter-term cycles that has a pronounced effect on UK inflation is the heliocentric movement of Venus. We have seen how the Jupiter–Saturn cycle has a particularly powerful effect every third opposition; in a similar way, the heliocentric movement of Venus shows the multiple cycle, in this case a fourfold one. But unlike the Jupiter–Saturn cycle, where simply every third opposition is emphasised, this cycle operates over four complete revolutions of Venus around the Sun. Each of the four revolutions, or heliocentric zodiac cycles, is distinctly different and the pattern only repeats itself after the fourth cycle has been completed. Fig. 3.11 shows how the cycle affects the UK Retail Price Index; again, this is a graph of the price level, not the rate of inflation. Each revolution of Venus around the Sun takes about 225 days, and so the whole fourfold cycle takes just under two-and-a-half years to complete.

During the first revolution of Venus around the Sun from 0-degrees Aries, prices fall relative to the long-term trend and so inflation is lower than average. Through the second and third Venus cycles, again until just before 0-degrees Aries, prices rise relative to the long-term trend and so inflation is above average. The fourth and final cycle is essentially flat, with prices rising at their long-term trend rate, and so there is no effect on inflation until the 240-degree point or the start of heliocentric Sagittarius. From this point, prices fall for the remaining third of this cycle, thus linking up with the fall in the first of the four cycles.

Using this Venus cycle provides us with an extremely useful short-term guide to the likely pattern of future inflation in the UK. The cycle shows that the low point of inflation is reached about halfway through the first of the four cycles, when prices are falling most rapidly relative to their long-term trend. In terms of UK inflation, this last happened in April 1993 and we expect this to mark a low point in inflation, *on the evidence of this cycle alone.* It goes without saying that the other inflation cycles, such as Saturn–Neptune, must be studied alongside this cycle, in order to arrive at a fully comprehensive picture of future inflationary trends.

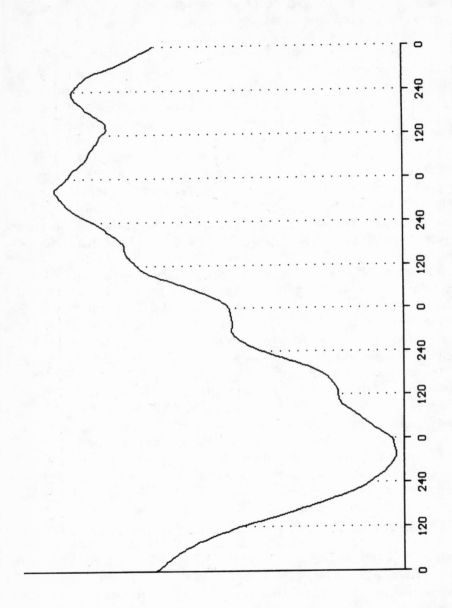

FIGURE 3.11: VENUS FOURFOLD HELIOCENTRIC CYCLE IN UK INFLATION

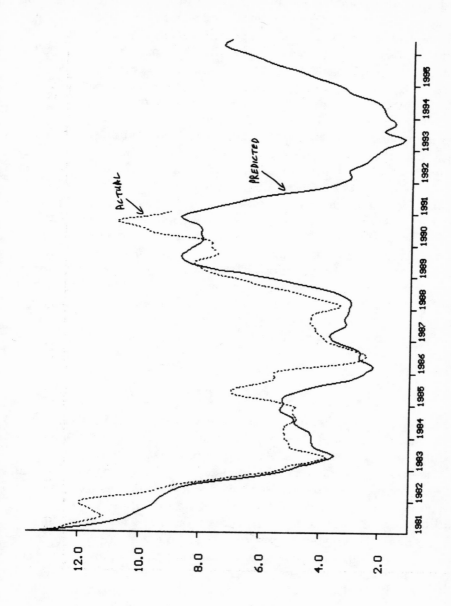

**FIGURE 3.12: UK ANNUAL PERCENTAGE CHANGE IN RPI
– ACTUAL AND PREDICTED**

As with economic activity, we can combine all the relevant long-term and short-term planetary cycles to produce an accurate forecast of future inflation levels in the UK, and there are several advantages to using an astrological approach when working with inflation. Firstly, financial astrology provides us with a picture of the long-term pattern of inflation that is hard to derive using other methods of forecasting. Secondly, this cycles-based approach has in the past produced a consistently reliable picture of inflation. As we found with the economy, different countries will show varying responses in their inflation rate in terms of planetary cycle turning-points and cycle 'shapes', so readers in other countries may like to experiment with the cycles and see how they affect their own economy.

Fig. 3.12 shows our prediction for UK inflation. We have used data up until early 1991 for this model, so the period following this date can be used for comparing the forecast with the known outcome. Working on the basis that the planetary effects will continue to operate as they have done in the past, inflation can be expected to reach a low point during 1993, following which it will rise *gradually* throughout 1994. Inflation could reach uncomfortably high levels again during 1995, perhaps even exceeding 6 per cent. It should be noted that this prediction is intended only as a general indication: the fine detail, particularly with regard to the timing of the low point, may vary from our prediction, but the general principle of a low in 1993, followed by a rise in inflation, should be borne out.

ASPECTS

Using planetary cycles enables us to form a broad picture of likely future trends in the economy, but in order to arrive at accurate predictions, a second factor, aspects, must also be taken into account.

The financial astrologers who worked with economic models earlier this century developed the theory that the astrological aspects between the outer planets, in particular Jupiter, Saturn and Uranus, can be matched with turning-points in the economy. Indeed, the post-war work of Williams, Rieder et al. has conclusively shown that the main movements in the world's economies do in fact tend to be accompanied by important planetary configurations between the outer planets. But, as we shall see, the mechanism by which aspects trigger financial movements is not as straightforward as the early financial astrologers initially believed.

It was originally thought that the classical 'good' aspects, such as the trine and sextile, directly correspond to periods of increasing prosperity and to upswings in the stock markets, and the traditional 'bad' aspects

– the square and opposition – could be linked with times of economic recession and a decline in confidence in both the economy and the markets. To a large extent this theory stands up, but detailed research revealed that using this rather simplistic approach failed to explain all the turning-points in the economy.

To be fair to the pioneers in this field, much of the early research was carried out before the 1940s and consequently encountered two major stumbling-blocks. First, detailed, accurate and sufficiently frequent (at least quarterly) data were not readily available at that time. The dearth of precise information on past economic performance meant that forecasts made on the basis of these data were therefore likely to be somewhat inaccurate. The second factor was that the planet Pluto, which exerts an extremely powerful and far-reaching influence on both the general economy and the markets, was not discovered until 1930, and it took several years for its effects on business activity to be fully assessed.

To illustrate how the aspects operate, it is useful to look at the economic events that correspond to the aspect patterns of Jupiter, Saturn and Uranus. Remembering that Jupiter relates to growth, expansion and enthusiasm, Saturn to restriction and cutbacks, and Uranus to sudden upsets or reversals of the status quo, we would expect to see squares or oppositions between these planets always marking a downturn in the economy. But detailed research has shown that this is not invariably the case. Figs. 3.1–3.3 show the index of UK GNP for the period 1894 to 1955 with the heliocentric aspects between Jupiter and Saturn, Jupiter and Uranus, and Saturn and Uranus marked. We see that although there are some correspondences, the match is inconsistent. As the effect of astrological aspects is too strong to be dismissed as mere chance, these irregularities need to be fully explained before we can see how aspects can provide an accurate timing mechanism for economic turning-points.

The graph shows that there is good agreement in 1900, where a low in GNP coincides with a Jupiter–Uranus conjunction, as would be expected, with the economy starting to grow. In 1914, when a Jupiter–Saturn trine is also in operation, the conjunction marks the start of a period of strong growth. Similarly, the next three conjunctions of Jupiter and Uranus, in 1927, 1941 and 1955, all occur during periods of growth.

The graph also shows a number of examples of clusters, i.e., groups of aspects, all of an unfavourable or 'hard' nature, which occurs around the end of 1930 and the beginning of 1931. Here, the Jupiter–Saturn opposition, the Jupiter–Uranus square and the Saturn–Uranus square all coincide. As would be expected, this was a time of major recession. In 1951, the Jupiter–Saturn opposition and Jupiter–Uranus square coincided again, producing the only downturn in the otherwise long and steady period of growth which lasted from 1947 to 1956. In these cases, hard aspects do coincide with adverse economic conditions, just as the classical theorists would have predicted.

Although matching aspects to economic events seems to work quite well for the Jupiter–Uranus conjunction, things are less clear-cut in the case of the opposition. Despite the fact that the 1907 opposition heralded a downturn in GNP and that of 1920 occurred during a period of falling GNP, in line with traditional astrological theory, the 1934 and 1948 oppositions took place, paradoxically, when the economy was growing! This anomaly, which few astrologers, with the exception of Williams, have attempted to resolve, was due to the fact that in 1907, the opposition was closely followed by the favourable influence of a Jupiter–Saturn trine. Similar Jupiter–Saturn trines also took place in 1934, where the favourable aspect occurred shortly before the Jupiter–Uranus opposition, and also in 1948, where both aspects occurred at almost the same time. Traditionally, trines are favourable aspects and would therefore be expected to raise GNP, whereas oppositions are unfavourable and would be expected to have the inverse effect of depressing it. So how should the situation be interpreted when both aspects occur at the same time? Do the aspects simply have the effect of cancelling each other out or is one stronger than the other for some reason? As is so often the case in financial astrology, the answer to these questions lies in broadening out the picture to take additional factors into consideration.

If we take the case of 1907, the Jupiter–Uranus opposition seemed to predominate and the subsequent Jupiter–Saturn trine was nullified. In 1934 and 1948, however, the Jupiter–Saturn trine seemed to win out over the Jupiter–Uranus opposition. At first sight, there does not appear to be any good reason why one particular aspect should act more strongly at certain times than at others. Certainly, no single causal factor can be identified if each scenario is interpreted solely in terms of the aspects occurring at the time. In fact, the explanation for these anomalies can only be found by looking to another factor to see how, in each instance, the growth-inducing trines or recession-inducing oppositions are being strengthened or weakened. That factor is the national chart – in this case the chart for the UK – and the way the transiting aspects link into that chart. Before looking at how aspects can be modified in this way, it will be useful to explore the concept of national charts in greater detail.

NATIONAL CHARTS

National charts are horoscopes which are drawn up for nations, as opposed to individuals or companies, and are based on the principle of setting up a chart for a state or nation, using the date and time the state was founded as a 'birth-time'. These national charts can be used to predict social and political events as well as financial movements, and a whole separate branch of astrology, known as mundane astrology, is devoted to analysing and predicting the cycles of socio-economic and political change. Until the early years of this century financial astrology was classed as a sub-branch of mundane astrology. Since that time, however, the whole area of financial astrology and its cycles-based analysis has expanded to the extent that it now forms a separate field of study in itself.

The detailed interpretation of national charts, which forms the basis of mundane astrology, lies beyond the scope of this book, as it is a highly complex field requiring a much deeper knowledge of astrology than we assume here. But since national charts can tell us a great deal about the likely economic events that will befall a country, and also help us to assess the impact of transiting aspects, they do form an essential tool of financial astrology. As a general rule, when predicting the economic outlook for any given country, we must always consider that country's national chart, for this provides an insight into how the transiting aspects are likely to operate. For this reason we must briefly consider the way aspects can be strengthened or weakened by their links into the chart for the country being considered.

Agreeing the precise time at which a nation is 'born' is not always a straightforward affair, but can sometimes give rise to continuing controversy, as in the case of the US chart. As historian-astrologer Nick Campion points out, at least three different charts for the United States of America are currently in common use and a small industry has arisen among astrologers seeking to make their reputations by proposing new charts or seeking to rectify existing ones! In this chapter, however, we will confine our discussion to the UK national chart, shown in Fig. 3.13. This is a far less controversial chart, since the 1801 Act of Union is generally agreed as the point at which the modern state came into being. Since the Act of Union is a piece of legislation, it also has the benefit of having an exact time and place, and is widely accepted among astrological researchers as the basis for the UK national chart.

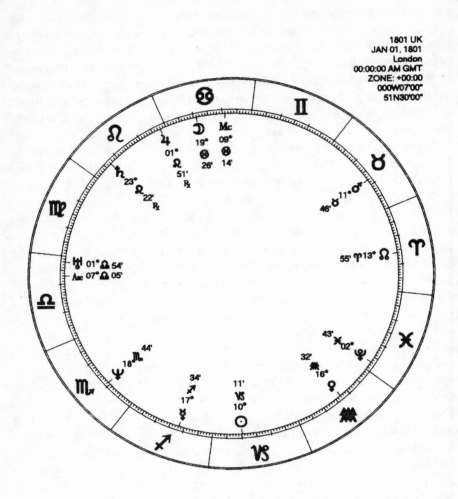

1801 UK
JAN 01, 1801
London
00:00:00 AM GMT
ZONE: +00:00
000W07'00"
51N30'00"

FIGURE 3.13: UK NATIONAL CHART

We have seen that when more than one transiting aspect occurs at the same time sometimes one aspect will tend to have a stronger effect on the country's economy than the other. If we take the three cases discussed above of a Jupiter–Uranus opposition occurring at the same time as a Jupiter–Saturn trine, we can see how the strengthening or weakening effect of links to the national chart actually worked out in practice. We will use the geocentric positions and aspects for this, as is usual when working with a chart. Note that we are interested in very close contacts to the chart, that is aspects between the transiting planets and the chart's planets that have a small orb.

Looking first at the 1906–7 series of aspects (and remembering that because of the retrograde effect the same aspect is formed a number of times), we find the links are as follows.

The Jupiter–Uranus opposition is very strong because the second time it occurs, with Jupiter at 7 ♋ 42 and Uranus at 7 ♑ 42, it is exactly square the UK Ascendant; and the final occurrence has Uranus at 12 ♑ 04 conjunct the UK Sun. These contacts highlight the opposition and link it to the UK through the national chart. The Jupiter–Saturn trines, on the other hand, are not so prominent. There is a link between Jupiter and the chart Midheaven, but the emphasis is less marked and so the opposition is stronger than the trine. Consequently, the overall effect in this case was to depress the economy.

In 1934 the Jupiter–Uranus opposition made no close contacts to the UK chart and so was not emphasised at all. The Jupiter–Saturn trine, on the other hand, had some very strong links: Jupiter sextile and Saturn opposing the UK's Saturn. Here the trine was the stronger transiting aspect and so it had a strong positive effect on the UK economy, which resulted in an upturn in GNP.

Finally, looking at the 1948 case we again find the Saturn aspecting the UK Saturn. The final trine is particularly strong, with the Jupiter exactly square the UK Ascendant. The opposition makes some contacts the first two times it occurs, but the final occurrence makes no contacts at all to the national chart. As in 1934, the overall emphasis is on the links between the Jupiter–Saturn trine and the UK national chart, rather than the links from the opposition of Jupiter and Uranus. Again the result was a strong trine and a consequent rise in GNP.

A different kind of aspect effect is shown by the very sharp upward turn in GNP in 1921. This coincided with a Jupiter–Saturn conjunction which operated as a trigger to a slow-moving Uranus–Pluto trine. The positions referred to in the UK chart are worth analysing:

	Jupiter conj Saturn	**Uranus trine Pluto**	
12.3.1921		6 ♓ 48	6 ♋ 48
25.7.1921		9 ♓ 01	9 ♋ 01
10.9.1921	26 ♍ 36 26 ♍ 36		
6.2.1922		8 ♓ 18	8 ♋ 18
17.9.1922		11 ♓ 06	11 ♋ 06
27.12.1922		10 ♓ 16	10 ♋ 16

The trine is repeated five times, which frequently happens with transits of the very slow-moving planets. The Pluto position is repeatedly conjunct the UK natal Midheaven and opposes the natal Sun, with Uranus trining the Midheaven and sextile the Sun. This is a very powerful configuration which links in strongly to the UK national chart and is a basically favourable configuration. The Jupiter–Saturn conjunction does not make a major aspect to the chart, but does however form an almost exact 135-degree aspect to natal Mars. The 135-degree aspect is not classified as a major aspect, but often has the effect of triggering other aspects in the shorter term. Thus contacts to Mars frequently operate as 'energisers' of aspects, reinforcing them and, as in this case, providing a short-term timing indication by triggering the longer-term favourable Uranus–Pluto trine and showing exactly when its effects will be reflected by a positive move in the economy.

Earlier, when looking at graphs of the UK cycles, it appeared that the traditional aspect points of the square, opposition, trine, etc. were not strongly marked. This apparent contradiction is due to the way the graphs were put together and should now be explained. In constructing the graphs, we averaged the cycles over a number of occurrences, so that taking UK GNP for the period 1830–1988, say, we are using 11 complete Jupiter–Uranus cycles to produce our average cycle graph. During some of these cycles, the first 90-degree square of the cycle will contact a sensitive point in the natal chart; during others, it will not. Thus on some occasions this square will be emphasised and override other factors; on other occasions, the square itself will be overshadowed by other factors. The result is to average out the effect of the square, which therefore does not show up strongly as part of the cycle.

Research has shown that aspects are important determinants of economic turning-points and that the traditional attributes of aspects seem to hold: squares and oppositions decrease economic activity; trines and sextiles increase it. But the aspects cannot be considered in isolation and must always be related back to the national chart. Different countries have different charts and so aspects between the outer planets will affect each country to a greater or lesser degree, depending on how strongly they link into the national chart. The national chart serves to 'ground' the aspects and also provides important insights into which countries are likely to be most affected by a particular planetary pattern.

Studying the way aspects between the outer planets link into the national chart is the best way of evaluating the relative strength of each aspect and thereby predicting how they are likely to influence the economy. Experience shows that the type of contact (hard or flowing aspect) made to the natal chart seems to be less important than the fact that a close contact has been made.

ASPECTS REVISITED: FINE-TUNING PREDICTIONS FOR THE UK ECONOMY

Aspects clearly have an important role to play in helping to predict the turning-points of economic activity, especially when they contact a country's national chart. In Fig. 3.9 we set up a prediction for UK GNP based on the UK planetary cycles, which suggested that the UK economy would falter in 1994 before growth resumed in 1995. Broadening out the astrological perspective to take account of the aspects in operation over the same time-period – and their relationship to the UK chart – puts the picture in a slightly different light and suggests that recovery will begin sooner rather than later.

In April and again in August 1994, there will be a Jupiter–Saturn trine, which will tend to promote and encourage the recovery. The exact positions are:

	Jupiter	**Saturn**
28.4.1994	10 ♏ 00	10 ♓ 00
28.8.1994	9 ♏ 19	9 ♓ 19

Looking at the UK chart, we see that both Jupiter and Saturn are trining the natal Midheaven. This contact is exact on the second occasion and both are also sextile the natal Sun (again exact on the second occasion). The Jupiter–Saturn trine will be strengthened by these contacts and will therefore tend to curb the slight downturn predicted by using our cycles approach. On this basis, sustained growth could therefore start in mid-1994 rather than 1995.

In this chapter, we have seen how cycles, aspects and national charts all have a crucial role to play in helping to forecast the likely future twists and turns of the economy. Our model used to produce predictions for the UK economy was largely based on the slower-moving cycles of the outer planets. In the case of the stock market, however – our next topic of investigation – it is the faster-moving planets and their cycles that play the most important role in helping us to stay one step ahead of events.

4

Predicting the Stock Market: Tools and Techniques

Institutional and private investors alike need hardly be reminded of the desirability of being able to make precise predictions of major upward and downward movements in the stock market well in advance. The ability to buy and sell at the right moment is the foundation-stone upon which fortunes can be made or lost. Although, as we have seen, the economy and stock market now act far more independently of each other than was the case, for example, during the 1930s, a crisis in the markets can still have considerable economic and political repercussions. The sudden falls of Black Monday in October 1987 that sent a chill wind through the world's markets were predicted a year in advance by British astrologers and had a distinctly adverse effect on confidence. In the stock market, as in no other area of business activity, the precise timing of decisions to buy and sell is of the essence. As we shall see, forecasting the markets is a field where financial astrology is proving itself to be increasingly accurate, effective and potent.

Financial astrology can be considered a form of cyclical analysis, which is one of the four main financial forecasting techniques currently in use on both sides of the Atlantic – the others being fundamental analysis, technical analysis and guessing. Since the late 1980s, an increasing number of market analysts and traders have begun to use astrology as a trading tool. So much so that the major Association of Market Analysts recently voted to include astrology as an accepted trading approach – largely at the request, incidentally, of its Japanese members. It is interesting to note that although financial astrology is being increasingly used by both American and British businesses, it is still more widely employed in the United States, where entrepreneurs and investors are noted for their thoroughgoing pragmatism and practicality. The stateside motto in this case, as always, is, 'If it works, use it!'

Stock market astrology, like all the other applications of financial astrology discussed in this book, is based solely on practical experience and detailed observation of the past effects of particular astrological patterns. One well-known and respected market trader who successfully uses astrology for forecasting the markets is Bill Meridian, who is consulted by the Sheikh of Abu Dhabi and writes a regular financial newsletter with an astrological slant. In association with US-based Robert Hand, he has also developed an astrological trading tool, the computer programme Astro-Analyst, which gives the trader the ability to analyse the effect on the market of different planetary cycles and combinations of cycles. Also in America, both Henry Weingarten of the New York School of Astrology and the late Neil Michelsen have established investment funds run exclusively along astrological lines.

Although research into the way astrology affects the market is still being carried out, and financial astrologers admit that their knowledge of this field is far from complete, they have nevertheless produced some impressive stock market forecasts over recent years. Mike Harding and Charles Harvey identified both the day of the crash of 19 October 1987 and the subsequent bottom of 11 November. In a press release of December 1989, Henry Weingarten pinpointed the Japanese stock market crash of early 1990. We have already seen how Graham Bates, the co-author of this book, also pinpointed the Wall Street Mini-Crash of 15 November 1991, which no forecaster using more conventional techniques managed to identify.

To an even greater extent than with the forecasting work carried out on the economy, the refinement of astrological techniques for predicting the swings and turns of the stock market relies heavily on the use of computers, and it is easy to see why, when one pauses to consider the sheer volume of data involved. In order to gain sufficient information on the workings of the various astrological effects, it is necessary to use at least 40 years' worth of data from the market. In an average year there are around 250 trading days in the main stock exchanges of the world and in order to study planetary effects their positions must be calculated for each of those days. With 40 years of data one can see that no less than 10,000 sets of daily positions must be calculated in order to study the market in depth! The sheer volume of calculation involved in stock market astrology was sufficient to deter most astrologers from embarking on this kind of in-depth investigation until the dawn of the computer age, with one notable exception – the redoubtable W. D. Gann.

As we have seen, W. D. Gann was an avid chartist and practitioner of astrology. Throughout the 1920s, Gann's *Annual Forecast* was widely read by American investors, and in November 1928 he predicted that the end of the great bull market in stocks would take place on 3 September 1929. He added the chilling observation that he felt the greatest panic in history would follow. In *The Great Crash 1929*, the definitive work on the events of those years, J. K. Galbraith wrote, 'On September 3rd, by common consent, the great bull market of the nineteen-twenties came to an end' – thus substantiating Gann's prediction with the wisdom of hindsight only history can vouchsafe.

Gann's subsequent publication, *Wall Street Selector*, which appeared in June 1930, featured a chapter entitled 'Investors Panic', which described conditions just as they occurred during the troubled years of 1931–3. 'The coming investors' panic will be the greatest in history ... once they [investors] get scared, which they will after years of decline, then the selling will be so terrific that no buying power can withstand it.' Gann penned these prophetic words in April 1930, when the Dow-Jones Industrial Average was at 297.50. By July 1932 it had plummeted to 40.50.

Impressive as these predictions are, readers should remember that fore-casting the market is a highly complex process, and there is no universal astrological formula that can be mechanically applied to suit all occasions. What this book can do, however, is to provide a set of useful astrological techniques based on hard practical evidence of past market performance, which when applied correctly, will undoubtedly improve any trader's abil-ity to make successful stock market predictions.

Although few latter-day traders would have the skill and patience to apply Gann's highly complicated techniques, their trading skills cannot fail to be enhanced by utilising the same astrological principles which were such an important part of his work.

A further word of caution is in order at this point. Experience has shown that there are so many different astrological factors that affect the market that it is extremely dangerous to rely on any one cycle or other factor – such as an eclipse or planetary aspect – alone when formulat-ing a decision to trade. Just as when we looked at the economy – and perhaps even more so in the markets – it is vital to consider the whole picture and to take as many factors as possible into consideration, time-consuming though this process may be. As we shall see, some cycles and factors act very strongly indeed and might initially seem to be so reliable that they could be used in isolation, but it is important to be aware that there are times when even the strongest cycles are over-whelmed by other factors. When it comes to the stock market, therefore, simplicity is not an approach to be encouraged. Comprehensive though our treatment of stock market astrology in these pages is, it is not totally exhaustive, due to limitations of space, and there are yet more cycles and factors not listed here which can also be used to produce market forecasts. (Readers with a special interest in the markets should refer to the recommendations for further reading in the Directory of Resources.)

The astrological picture of the stock market described in these chap-ters may seem exceedingly complicated, with its plethora of different interrelated factors to consider. But those who genuinely wish to improve their trading performance will find that studying these factors will, in the long run, be most rewarding. The methods outlined here include the main tools currently being used by financial astrologers to produce reliable trading indicators, as well as the most up-to-date and advanced techniques discovered in the course of Graham Bates' ongoing research.

Stock market astrology involves using some familiar principles already encountered when creating forecasts for the economy and to a certain extent the same general rules apply. The astrological cycles that govern the movements of the stock market provide an overall description of what is happening and show whether the market is likely to rise or fall. But for the exact timing of market moves, we must examine the aspect patterns. The national and stock exchange chart for the particular country under consideration are also key factors that should be considered.

When looking at the economy, we were largely concerned with the effects of longer-term cycles, such as the Jupiter–Saturn cycle. The astrology of the stock market, however, is largely determined by shorter-term cycles and by the aspect points of certain outer planet cycles. One of the major slower-moving cycles that powerfully influences the market is the Saturn–Pluto cycle, where the square aspect has been found to have a severely bearish effect on the UK market. These slower-moving cycles usually need to be activated by a fast-moving planet or 'trigger', such as the Sun or Moon, before they can take effect. As these 'triggers' are extremely important for timing stock market movements, we will be examining them in considerable detail. Astrological phenomena such as eclipses and planetary stations can also have important and sometimes dramatic effects on the stock market, and we will be examining these in depth in Chapter 5.

MULTIPLE CYCLES: A UNIQUE APPROACH

Finally, one of the most important techniques for pinpointing market turning-points is that of multiple cycles, which involves looking at how two planets behave over their double, triple and even quadruple cycles. This important concept represents a significant departure from conventional financial astrology, (which has generally confined itself to looking at simple cycles), and was pioneered by W. D. Gann in the course of his work with the Jupiter–Saturn triple cycle, discussed in Chapter 3. The use of multiple cycles, i.e., looking at the market's movement not just over one cycle of any two planets, but over two, three or even four cycles, has been specially developed by Graham Bates, one of the co-authors of this book, and this unique approach to forecasting is an important contribution to our understanding of this complex field.

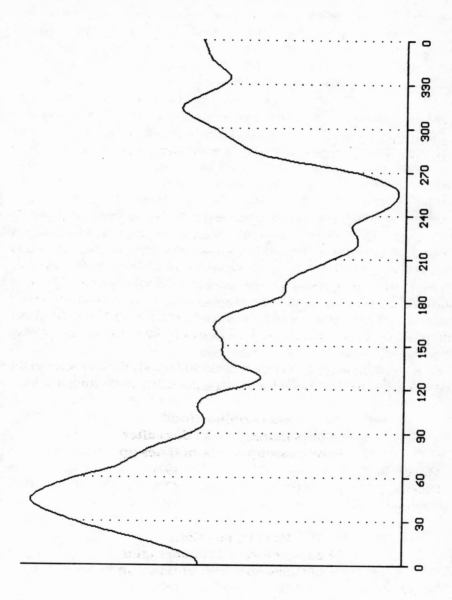

FIGURE 4.1: SUN CYCLE IN UK STOCK MARKET

The Sun's Cycle

Our discussion of stock market cycles begins with the Sun. When dealing with the economy, we found that cycles of 10 years, 20 years or even longer were useful in predicting the timing of growth and recession, but in the stock market these long-term cycles offer little insight. For example, a 10-year 'up' period followed by a 10-year 'down' would, even if it moved the market plus and minus 20 per cent (e.g., 600 points on an index at 3,000), only produce a 60-point annual move, amounting to a paltry 5 points a month! The astrology of the stock market requires that we study planetary movements from a much more short-term perspective.

The Sun is the best known of all the shorter-term cycles and Fig. 4.1. shows how this cycle unfolds in the market throughout the year. Our graph has been derived in the same way as those used in Chapter 3, by averaging out many occurrences of the cycle, in this instance using 47 years of UK stock market data. We can see that the UK stock market tends to hit a low point when the Sun is around the middle of Sagittarius (in December), between 240 and 270 degrees on the graph. The market then rises until the Sun reaches the middle of Aquarius in early February. This corresponds to the well-known 'January Rally', but it actually starts well in advance of the New Year, in December rather than January.

The second part of the rise takes place when the Sun enters Aries on 20 or 21 March and lasts until it reaches the middle of Taurus in early May. This May peak is the basis of the well-known market saying, 'Sell in May and go away', and although the peak does not invariably happen, it has taken place so many times over the last 47 years that the graph clearly shows this time-honoured advice to be well-founded – at least as far as the average performance of the market is concerned. The graph also shows that *on average* the market fall after the May peak continues through the rest of the year until the low point in December, albeit with minor rallies along the way.

The Sun's Four-Year Cycle

Considered from a different perspective, the Sun's cycle also produces one of the strongest forecasting tools yet discovered by financial astrologers. In the same way that the Jupiter–Saturn cycle has a particularly powerful effect on the economy at every third opposition point, the 'January Rise' of the Sun's cycle also tends to follow a regular multiple cycle. Here every fourth cycle of the Sun shows a stronger than average rise in the first part of the year. Not only is the rise more pronounced than average, but it also tends to carry on for longer and frequently lasts into June.

This four-year solar cycle is one of the most powerful forecasting techniques UK traders can use, for if we look at the post-war history of the UK stock market, taking the period from 22 December in the previous year to 1 May in the year in question, *every single* fourth year demonstrates a marked rise. Recent years which have featured this rise include 1975 – where it was particularly spectacular! – 1979, 1983, 1987 – another notably strong early year rise, but one which sadly came to grief – and 1991. Since the four-year solar cycle has worked every single time since 1945, we predict that the next such strong early-year rally will take place in 1995.

Further proof of the predictive power of this cycle is the fact that our 46-year data sample also shows 12 occasions when there was a fall from December to May, but none of these took place in years when the four-year solar cycle would suggest the trend should have been strongly upwards. The four-year solar cycle is an extremely powerful tool indeed and provides a telling introduction to the concept of assessing events in the market by means of multiple cycles.

The Cycles of Mercury and Venus

Two other important annual cycles feature the planets Mercury and Venus. When viewed geocentrically, these planets are always close to the Sun, Mercury usually lying within 28 degrees of the Sun and Venus within 48 degrees. Due to the phenomenon of retrogradation, which will be explored more fully in due course, the cycles of these two planets are irregular, being sometimes shorter than a year, sometimes longer. The difference in position between Venus and the Sun, in particular, provides a good way of timing market turning-points.

Fig. 4.2 shows the effect of the Venus cycle on the UK stock market. Comparing this with the Sun's cycle, we can see that while both cycles hit a low point in Sagittarius and have roughly the same overall shape, the Venus cycle shows a strong fall in Libra and Scorpio. The timing of this downturn varies from year to year, but generally takes place in the period between September and early December. This positioning of Venus in late Libra and early Scorpio usually spells bad news for the UK stock market. Experience shows that it produces falls with such regularity that financial astrologer Dan Pallant cites it as one of the key timing indicators for any autumn fall. In October 1987, for instance, at the

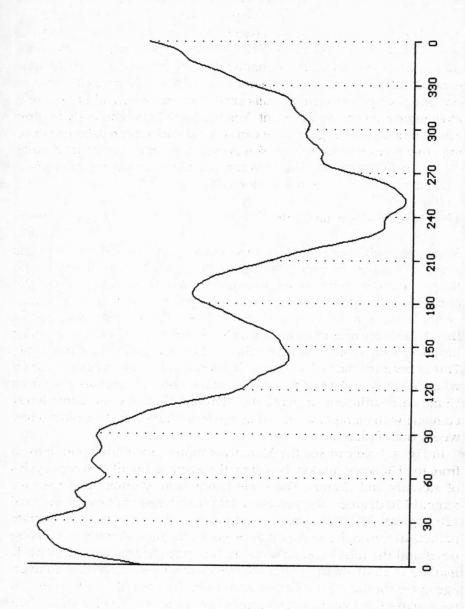

FIGURE 4.2: VENUS CYCLE IN UK STOCK MARKET

time of the Black Monday crash, Venus was at 10 degrees of Scorpio, having entered that sign on Saturday 10 October. During the entire period over which Venus transited Scorpio that year, the market saw strong falls most days before the final cataclysmic crash on 19 October. Two years later, Venus entered Scorpio on 12 September 1989, which marked the start of a 300-point fall in the market. The entry of Venus into Scorpio is not a sufficiently powerful factor to produce falls *by itself* and does not therefore produce strong falls each year. But when additional negative indicators are also present, Venus in late Libra and early Scorpio acts as a catalyst or 'trigger', that can activate and reinforce the pre-existing downward trend. The day Venus enters Scorpio is often marked by a one day fall in the market – even when there is no longer-term negative pattern to trigger into a major longer lasting fall.

The Mercury–Uranus Cycle

Significant insights into market moves can also be obtained by looking at the cycles between the fast-moving planets – the Sun, Mercury and Venus – and the slow-moving outer planets. These planetary cycles produce interesting differences in timing compared with the simple annual cycles of the Sun, Mercury and Venus. One such planetary pairing that has proved very useful in forecasting is the Mercury–Uranus cycle, which produces a far stronger effect on the market than the Sun–Uranus cycle. This is because the small timing differences of a few weeks between when Mercury and when the Sun are at the same angular distance from Uranus are sufficient to make the Mercury–Uranus cycle consistently coincide with market moves, while the Sun–Uranus cycle is often a few weeks out of phase.

In Fig. 4.3 we can see the Mercury–Uranus geocentric cycle derived from the UK stock market, based on the average for all post-war cycles of Mercury and Uranus. The cycle is not quite symmetric; it rises for around 150 degrees, then enters a flat phase before falling for the final 120 degrees. The traditional aspect patterns do not appear to operate particularly strongly, as the cycle peaks 15 degrees after the opposition point and the trines and squares of the cycle's latter part are scarcely marked at all. It should be remembered, however, that this is an average cycle for the whole period and, as in the case of the economy, if the squares link into the UK national chart or stock exchange chart, their effect will be particularly emphasised and they will act more strongly than during those years when no such contact is made.

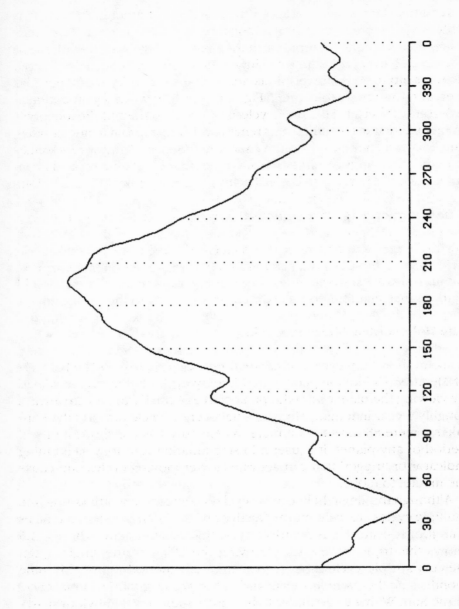

FIGURE 4.3: MERCURY–URANUS CYCLE IN UK STOCK MARKET

The Mercury–Uranus Double Cycle

The single cycle of Mercury and Uranus is useful as a predictive tool, but only seems to work for the UK stock market; it appears to have little value for predicting movements in the New York market. When seeking a more global technique that will highlight trends in an international context, far more interesting insights are to be obtained by looking at the Mercury–Uranus double cycle. Fig. 4.4 shows how the cycle operates when the effect of the single cycle has been discounted. Readers will immediately see that the cycle is remarkably uncompromising and clear-cut. It is exactly phased on the two conjunctions, rising very strongly from the first conjunction to the second and then falling away sharply for the second part of the cycle. The two most recent peaks of the double cycle were in early 1992 and early 1994.

Not only is the Mercury–Uranus double cycle one of the clearest market indicators, but it also affects the London and New York stock markets equally, unlike the market-specific single cycle. Using the multiple-cycle approach therefore not only allows us to discover powerful trading indicators, it also shows us the common connections between different world markets that are otherwise hard to discern.

The Heliocentric Mercury Cycle

A useful short-term cycle for market forecasting is the heliocentric cycle of Mercury. Unlike the geocentric Mercury cycles, which are obtained by viewing the planet from the perspective of the Earth and are always roughly a year in length, Mercury's heliocentric cycle (around the Sun) takes a mere 88 days to complete. As Mercury has the shortest orbital period of any planet, it is useful in stock market astrology as a timing indicator or 'trigger' that can activate slower-moving cycles and cause the market to move.

Although the single heliocentric cycle of Mercury is worth noting, the multiple cycles are even more effective and research has shown that, as with Jupiter–Saturn, it is the triple cycle that acts most strongly. Fig. 4.5 shows this triple cycle after removing the effect of the single cycle. Mercury's triple cycle around the Sun has a period of roughly nine months, and therefore moves in and out of phase with the annual cycle of the Sun. With a cycle through the zodiac there are no obvious marking points. With a two-planet cycle, the conjunction or opposition might provide the turning-points, but here it could be anywhere in the zodiac. In fact, heliocentric Virgo (150 to 180 degrees on the graph) seems to

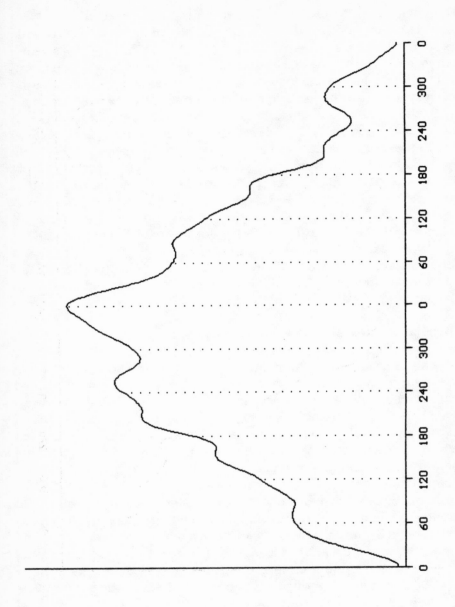

FIGURE 4.4: MERCURY–URANUS DOUBLE CYCLE IN UK STOCK MARKET

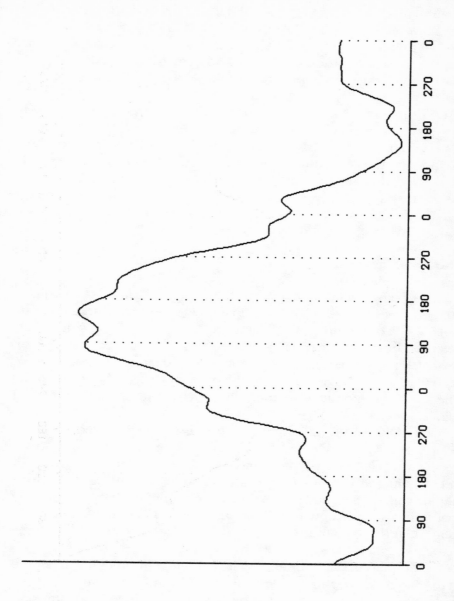

FIGURE 4.5: MERCURY HELIOCENTRIC TRIPLE CYCLE IN UK STOCK MARKET

be the important placement within the triple cycle of Mercury. The market tends to peak with heliocentric Mercury in Virgo of the middle cycle. From here it falls until Virgo of the third cycle; thus for one complete circuit of Mercury from Virgo back to Virgo, the market trends down. During the next circuit until Virgo of the first cycle, the market is flat. There are a few ups and downs, but no definite trend. From here the market trends up for the remainder of the first circuit and through to heliocentric Mercury in Virgo of the middle circuit.

This triple cycle and the single cycle are not tremendously strong movers of the market in themselves – the triple cycle can produce moves of around plus or minus 1.5 per cent – but can often be a powerful trigger for larger market turns. Mercury entered Virgo of the middle cycle on 6 March 1993 and the market made a high on 8 March. The rise to this date and the subsequent fall were in fact caused by a number of different factors coming together, but the heliocentric Mercury triple cycle was one of the final triggers that caused the market to peak.

The Sun–Mars Cycle

Another planetary cycle that provides trading indicators when considered both as a single and as a multiple cycle is the Sun–Mars cycle. The single cycle has a period of 25½ months. As shown in Fig. 4.6, it is characterised by a very sharp fall and almost immediate recovery. The fall in the UK market starts at the opposition (180 degrees) and stops at the second trine (240 degrees): the length of the fall is therefore 60 degrees. The rise is almost exactly the same length, 60 degrees from trine to final sextile.

Back in the 1970s, the astrologer Thomas Rieder discovered that the double Sun–Mars cycle had a pronounced effect on the Dow, so we tested the cycle to see if it produced a similar effect in the UK stock market. As with the Mercury–Uranus double cycle, we removed the effects of the single cycle, and Fig. 4.7 shows the result. Again, we see a cycle that trends sharply downward and then rises, with the difference that here the turning-point is not positioned on the conjunction, but some 30 degrees after.

The double cycle lasts around four years and three months (it peaked at the end of 1989), and consequently provides an interesting interaction with the Sun's four-year cycle. When the rising phase of the Sun–Mars double cycle coincides with the rising phase of the Sun's four-year cycle, as was the case in 1975, the result is a particularly sharp rise. Over time, the relative phase of two cycles varies. Sometimes the rising phases

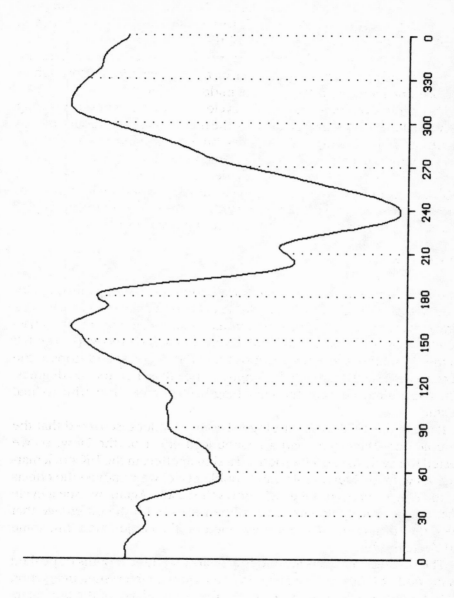

FIGURE 4.6: SUN–MARS CYCLE IN UK STOCK MARKET

Money and the Markets

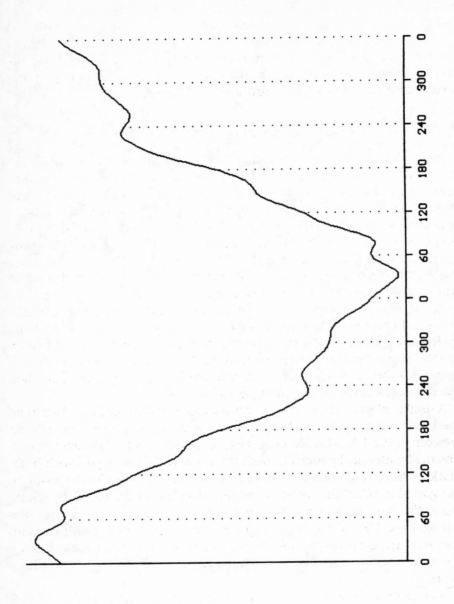

FIGURE 4.7: SUN–MARS DOUBLE CYCLE IN UK STOCK MARKET

coincide, reinforcing each other – as in 1975 – and on other occasions, the rising phase of one will coincide with the falling phase of the other and they cancel out. Awareness of these interweaving rhythms can provide traders with invaluable insights, although it should be noted that every year is different, since nothing in astrology ever exactly repeats itself. Each Sun–Mars interaction will therefore find all the other planetary cycles in varying positions and years like 1975, when the patterns were extremely clear-cut, are few and far between!

SINGLE AND MULTIPLE CYCLES

It must also be stressed again that different markets react to different cycles. Much astrological work has been published on the cycles that affect the US market, but British readers trading in the home market should always remember that most of the published research is market-specific and work carried out in the US market rarely works for the UK. Just as the pattern of growth and recession in the US is strongly influenced by the Moon's Node cycle (which has little effect on the UK), cycles that have a strong predictive capacity when applied to the UK stock market may not be any use at all for forecasting events in New York or Tokyo. Multiple cycles, however, tend to work rather better across different markets than single cycles. The simple cycle of the Sun, for instance, works well for the London stock market, but is much weaker in the US market. But when we look at the Sun's four-year cycle, not only does the US stock market show a strong rise every four years, but the rise takes place *in the same year* as the UK.

A similar effect can be observed with the Mercury–Uranus cycle. Although the basic single cycle can be seen to operate in both markets, it is far weaker in the US. The Mercury–Uranus double cycle, however, has a practically identical pattern in both the US and the UK, again with both markets rising and falling in the same years. Finally, conclusive proof of the global applicability of these multiple cycles can be found by looking at the Sun–Mars cycle. The single cycle operates differently in the UK and the US, being far stronger in the latter. When its effects are removed, the graph of the double cycle in the US (Fig. 4.8) shows exactly the same sequence as the UK – two rising years followed by two falling years.

As a general rule therefore, while single cycles, such as that of the Sun or Mercury–Uranus, tend to produce market-specific effects, multiple cycles, such as the Sun's four-year cycle and the Sun–Mars double cycle, have the capacity to cross national boundaries and provide stock

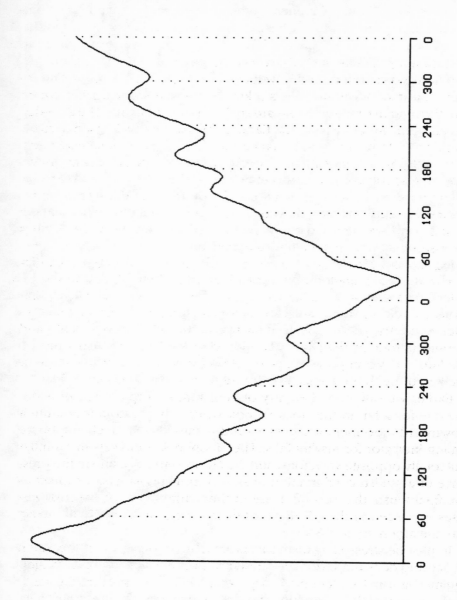

FIGURE 4.8: SUN–MARS DOUBLE CYCLE IN NEW YORK STOCK MARKET

market indicators that can often be applied across the board in both London and New York.

LUNAR INFLUENCES: FACT OR FICTION?

The influence of the Moon's 27-day cycle on terrestrial tides and mankind's emotions was scientifically proven centuries ago, and it's no surprise to learn that the Moon also plays a key role in the stock market where emotion and market sentiment are such important factors. The 27.3-day circuit of the Moon around the Earth is the shortest cycle used in stock market astrology, but its importance should not be underestimated. Just as with the heliocentric Mercury cycles, these rapidly moving cycles do not bring about significant market moves by themselves, but tend to act in tandem with the stronger, long-term factors that are concurrently influencing the market. When viewed as a planetary trigger or catalyst in the context of these longer-term cycles, the short-term cycle of the Moon is an important factor to take into account.

Fig. 4.9 shows that the 27-day lunar cycle demonstrates a similar pattern to the Sun's single cycle, with a high point being found in Pisces, Aries and Taurus – the solar cycle peaked in Taurus – and a low point in Scorpio, whereas the solar low point is positioned one sign later in Sagittarius. The remarkable fact that the Moon's 27-day cycle peaks and troughs in roughly the same places provides evidence that not only are the Sun and Moon powerfully connected, but also that the passage of the Sun through the zodiac is far more than a mere 'seasonal effect'.

Earlier we saw how the entry of Venus into Scorpio often provides the cue for a fall in the stock market when other factors indicating a downward movement are present and is thus an extremely important timing indicator for market falls. The Moon in Scorpio acts in a similar but totally opposite way, for when the Moon enters Scorpio in the presence of a bullish configuration of slower-moving planets, it can act as the final 'push' that sets off a rise in the market. One of the strongest rises ever seen in the UK market began on 6 January 1975, the exact day the Moon entered Scorpio.

It must be stressed again at this point that the presence of the Moon in Scorpio does not *cause* the market to rise, rather it acts as a triggering mechanism for other planetary factors. Before making trading decisions, it is essential to examine the whole planetary picture, for if there are no other factors present that would suggest a rise in the market, the passage of the Moon through Scorpio will not bring about a significant rise by itself – it needs something to work with, something to trigger off.

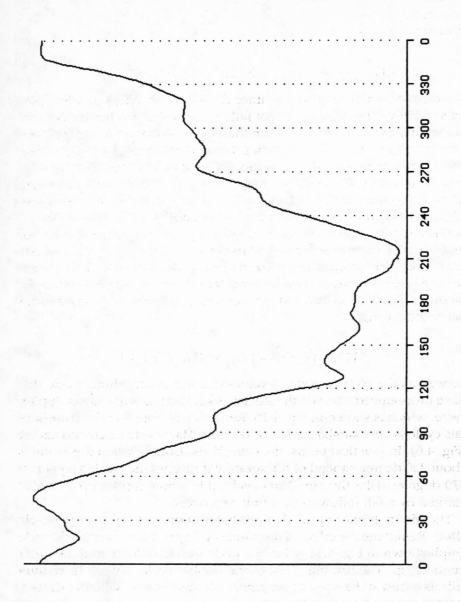

FIGURE 4.9: MOON CYCLE IN UK STOCK MARKET

Although, as we have seen, the short-term cycles of the Moon are cycles in their own right, they are not particularly tradable ones and the Moon's influence is most powerfully felt when it functions as a trigger for other, slower-moving planets.

THE SIGNIFICANCE OF SCORPIO

As we have seen, the entry of either the Moon or Venus into Scorpio can suddenly bring about a rise or fall in the market if other factors are present and experience has shown that this position in the zodiac is an extremely powerful one. According to conventional astrology, Pluto, which is the planetary ruler of Scorpio, is associated with issues of wealth, money, shared resources and power, and it's therefore most appropriate that this area of the zodiac should be linked to the stock markets. Although Scorpio cannot be linked with either exclusively bullish or bearish trends, research in recent years has yielded conclusive evidence that when Venus is in Scorpio the market is more likely to fall and when the Moon is in Scorpio the market is more likely to rise. It is always worthwhile watching the market carefully, therefore, when either the Moon or Venus enter Scorpio, or when major planetary configurations occur in that sign.

THE MOON–JUPITER CYCLE

As well as the Moon's zodiac cycle, there is a second lunar cycle that has a pronounced effect on the stock market and this is the Moon–Jupiter cycle, which is shown in Fig. 4.10. Readers will note that the pattern of this cycle is very similar to that of the Sun–Mars cycle discussed earlier (Fig. 4.6). In practical terms, the cycle rises strongly when the Moon is about 220 degrees ahead of Jupiter until it reaches the closing square at 270 degrees. Like the Sun–Mars cycle, this Moon–Jupiter cycle is also marked by a fall followed by a quick recovery.

The Moon–Jupiter cycle also produces an interesting multiple-cycle effect. Removing the effect of the single cycle produces the double cycle graph shown in Fig. 4.11, with one cycle trending down and the other trending up. The turning-point of the double cycle, where the market falls, is found at the opposition point – as was the case with the slower-moving Jupiter–Saturn triple cycle.

As well as the two lunar cycles discussed above, other cycles of the Moon also have an effect on the UK stock market. In particular the Sun–Moon interaction – the lunation cycle of New and Full Moons – has

Money and the Markets

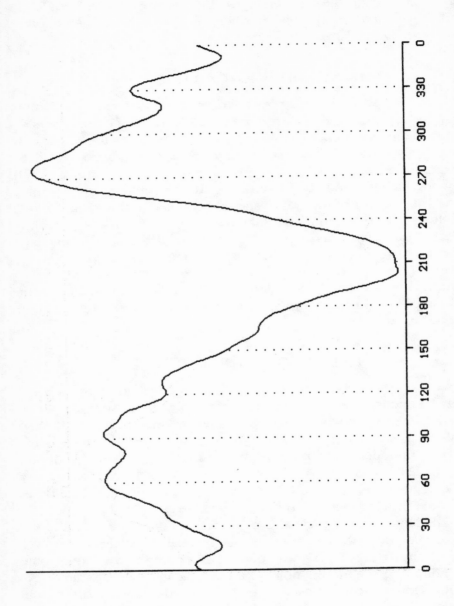

FIGURE 4.10: MOON–JUPITER CYCLE IN UK STOCK MARKET

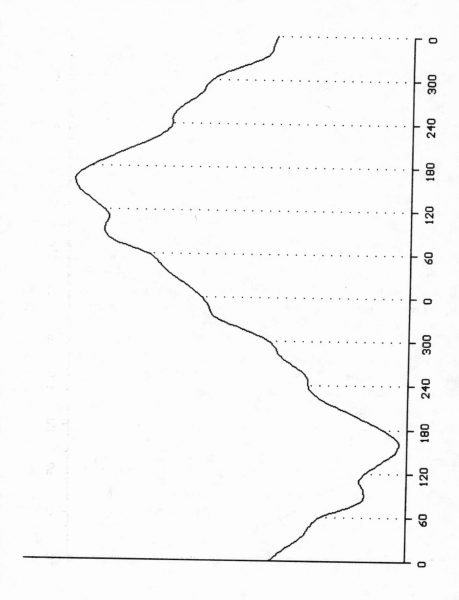

FIGURE 4.11: MOON–JUPITER DOUBLE CYCLE IN UK STOCK MARKET

a powerful role to play in activating slower-moving planetary cycles and it is to this fascinating phenomenon of 'triggering' that we shall now turn.

TRIGGERS

The use of the term 'trigger' is deliberate. We have described the way the Moon in Scorpio can trigger bullish indicators or Venus in Scorpio bearish ones, but it is the presence of the longer-term factors that is the really important point. Pulling the trigger of a gun that is not loaded produces no effect, aside from a short 'click'. In the same way, astrological triggers will have very little effect – and certainly produce no major market moves – if there are no longer-term factors ready and waiting to be triggered into action. One of the main astrological researchers in this complex field has been C. C. Matlock, whose important book *Man and Cosmos* (1977) explored the effect of planetary cycles on the Dow. In particular, his work looked at how the Sun's cycle provides a triggering and timing mechanism for the crucial Jupiter–Saturn cycle. Although Matlock's work was based on the Dow, similar effects are found in the UK market and so his research is worth exploring in some detail.

After looking at the Jupiter–Saturn cycle, much as we have done in the examples presented so far, Matlock carried out an important analysis of the role played by the Sun in triggering and timing this cycle. As a similar triggering effect occurs in the UK market, where the Sun triggers Jupiter–Saturn trines, we will look at this in some detail. For our analysis we will treat the two trines – when Jupiter is 120 degrees ahead of Saturn and when it is 240 degrees ahead (or 120 degrees behind) – separately, as their effects are different and they are triggered in different ways.

It is also worth noting that in many planetary aspect cycles, the two instances of the trine – or the square – seem to show this difference. The two trines or two squares behave very differently from the other, producing radically contrasting effects in the stock market. Finally, one aspect of the pair is often very much stronger in its effects than the other, so it is well worth noting when the 'strong' aspect is due to take place.

We will also see this effect when we come to consider the Saturn–Pluto squares which have such a marked influence on the UK stock market.

Triggering a Rise

The second trine in the Jupiter–Saturn cycle (Jupiter 240 degrees ahead of Saturn) produces a rise in the UK market and we shall examine this aspect pattern first. As is generally observed with slower-moving cycles, the rise does not take place when the aspect is exact but rather when it is activated by a faster-moving trigger. The trigger for both this trine and the 120 degree trine is the Sun. In the case of the 240-degree trine, the triggering takes place when the Sun opposes Saturn.

In 1954 a Jupiter–Saturn trine was in effect when the Sun opposed Saturn on 26 April, producing a strong rise over the next few weeks. Again in 1955, when the trine was still active, the Sun opposed Saturn on 9 May, again triggering a rise. The next Jupiter–Saturn trine 240 degrees ahead was in 1975, when the Sun–Saturn opposition was on 6 January. A spectacular rise ensued, when the market almost doubled within the space of a month!

The 1975 example serves to remind us once again how important it is to take the whole planetary picture into account. Jupiter was trining Saturn in January, a time when we would naturally expect the market to rise due to the effect of the Sun's annual cycle. In addition, 1975 was also one of the key 'rise' years in the Sun's four-year cycle, giving us further grounds for expecting the market to swing upwards. The Sun–Saturn

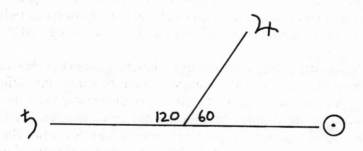

FIGURE 4.12

opposition triggered the Jupiter–Saturn trine into activation on 6 January and the final 'icing on the cake' was provided by the fact that the Moon also entered Scorpio on 6 January, adding yet another bullish factor to the planetary mix. The resulting rise was particularly strong since it was produced not just by one or two, but several positive astrological factors all coinciding at the same time, thus signalling that the market would not just rise, but would do so very sharply indeed. The next rising Jupiter–Saturn trine will be in 1994 and the Sun opposes Saturn that year on 1 September. This configuration does not automatically guarantee a rise, but as previous evidence points to a strong likelihood, we predict that the market will rise. Without the presence of all the other positive factors found in 1975, the rise will not be of such spectacular proportions – but there are no strong downward influences present in September 1994 either, so a reasonable rise is highly probable.

Triggering a Fall

The first trine in the Jupiter–Saturn cycle, when Jupiter is 120 degrees ahead of Saturn, has the reverse effect to the 240-degree trine: it causes the stock market to fall. In this case, the trine is triggered by the Sun when it opposes Jupiter, rather than Saturn. In 1948, Jupiter made this 120-degree trine to Saturn and the Sun opposed Jupiter on 15 June. The market promptly fell.

The next time Jupiter made this trine to Saturn was in 1967. The Sun opposed Jupiter on 20 January, but as this was a key 'rise' year in the Sun's four-year cycle and January is an 'up' month in the Sun's annual cycle, the trine caused little damage. This example further illustrates the importance of taking all the relevant cycles into consideration. The fact that these different planetary patterns came together at the same time caused them to cancel out and the result was a fairly neutral month in the markets; in fact a small rise occurred rather than a fall.

Twenty years later, Jupiter made this falling trine to Saturn in 1987 and the Sun opposed Jupiter on Sunday 18 October, an historic day in stock market annals, since the following trading day was 19 October – otherwise known as Black Monday. The presence of the Sun–Jupiter trigger was the key factor that led leading British astrologers to pinpoint 19 October as the day when the 1987 UK bull market would end. In addition, Venus had entered Scorpio a week earlier, also suggesting the likelihood of a fall. As we would expect with such a large move, many other astrological factors were at work behind the scenes on Black Monday and we will explore these in more detail in Chapter 5.

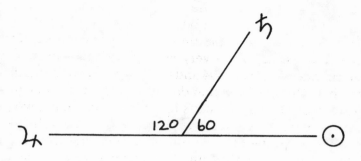

FIGURE 4.13

Readers might care to note that this falling Jupiter–Saturn trine occurs again in 2007 and the Sun opposes Jupiter on 5 June. The trine is not very exact, so we don't expect a very large downward movement, but a fall will certainly take place.

The Saturn–Pluto Cycle: The Sun–Moon Trigger

Another long-term cycle that exerts a powerful effect on the UK stock market is the Saturn–Pluto cycle, where the square aspects – particularly the closing square of Saturn to Pluto (Saturn 270 degrees ahead of Pluto) – generally signal a decline. Although both squares (Saturn 90 degrees ahead of Pluto and Saturn 270 degrees ahead of Pluto) signal a downturn in the UK market, this cycle shows very clearly the phenomenon of one square acting more strongly than the other – the 270-degree square being, in this case, the more powerful. As the Saturn–Pluto cycle involves two slow-moving planets, a fast-moving trigger is required to bring the square to life, the necessary planetary trigger in this instance being provided by the interaction of the Sun and Moon.

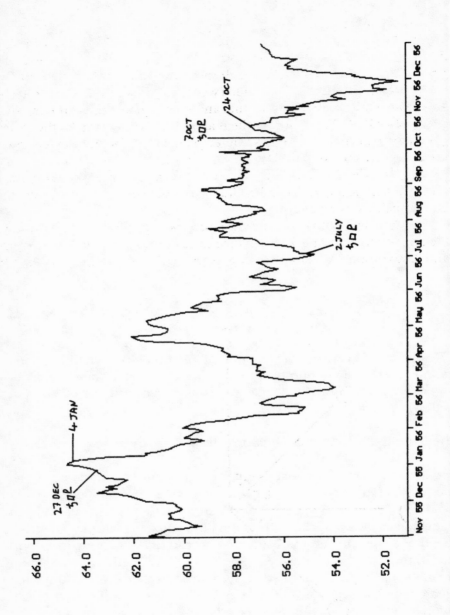

FIGURE 4.14: UK STOCK MARKET 1955–6; SATURN–PLUTO SQUARES

Due to retrograde motion, each of the examples we shall look at features three squares of each type during the space of a year. Fig. 4.14 shows the market during the 1955–6 square, when Saturn was 90 degrees ahead of Pluto. The dates of the squares are marked: 27 December 1955, 2 July 1956 and 7 October 1956. Note that the market falls did not exactly coincide with the squares; indeed, the middle square, in July 1956, marks a low point, not the start of a fall. Two major break points in the market are also noted, just after the first and third squares on 4 January and 24 October 1956. The timing of the market falls is not given by the exact planetary aspect between these outer planets, but by the triggering of the aspect by the Sun and Moon.

On 4 January 1956, a Quarter Moon occurred, with the Sun 90 degrees ahead of the Moon, which linked into the Saturn–Pluto square to create a remarkably exact pattern.

The Moon falls halfway between Saturn and Pluto, and these two interlocking square patterns between the Sun and Moon and between Saturn and Pluto brought the slow-moving square to life, initiating a two-month

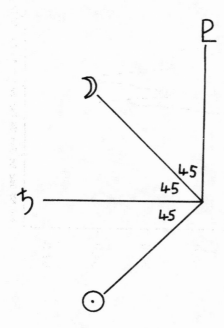

FIGURE 4.15

fall, starting on the very day the aspect was triggered. Such a tight inter-weaving of slow- and fast-moving planets is quite rare. The second Saturn–Pluto square in July was not triggered in this way by the Sun and Moon, and so no fall took place at that time. But another symmetric pattern did occur on 24 October 1956, when the Sun and Moon again linked in to the Saturn–Pluto square.

The Sun and Moon are 120 degrees apart, with Pluto exactly halfway between them. Mercury is also just past the point midway between Saturn and Pluto, adding further weight to their square. Again the triggering marked, to the day, the start of the fall.

Our second example features the 1973–4 stock market fall, which coincided with the ominous closing square of the Saturn–Pluto cycle, which is the more powerful of the two. Fig. 4.17 shows the period of the three occurrences of the square that year. The first two squares on 14 September and 7 October 1973 had little effect until a triggering Full Moon on Saturday 10 November set off a sharp fall on the very next trading day, Monday 12 November.

The symmetric effect of the Moon opposing the Sun at 45 degrees to both Saturn and Pluto activated the square, and again we see the exact date of a fall being given by the triggering configuration. The last square in the series was not triggered in this way and so no major break in

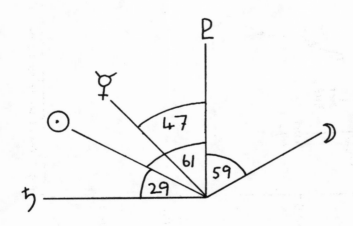

FIGURE 4.16

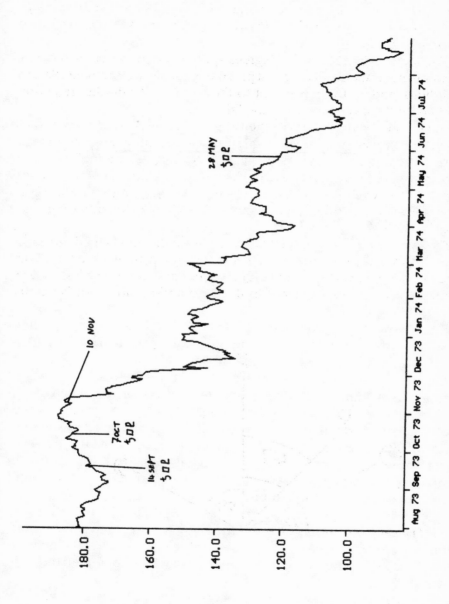

FIGURE 4.17: UK STOCK MARKET 1973–4; SATURN–PLUTO SQUARES

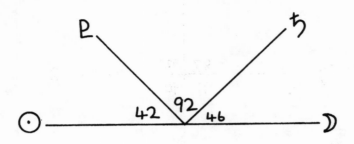

FIGURE 4.18

the market occurred. But other negative factors prolonged the decline until the end of the year when it sprang upwards again in January 1975 under the influence of the triggered Jupiter–Saturn trine.

Our final example explores the 1993–4 Saturn–Pluto squares, when Saturn was making its 90-degree square to Pluto on 20 March 1993, 9 October 1993 and 2 January 1994. Looking back to May 1992, when the square aspect was still forming, with Saturn not quite 90 degrees ahead of Pluto, we can see that although the aspect did not quite become exact before Saturn turned retrograde and only came within two to three degrees of the square, a powerful activation occurred on 9 May, when a Quarter Moon made the pattern shown in Fig. 4.19.

The four squares formed the difficult astrological configuration known as a 'Grand Cross', which activated the latent Saturn–Pluto square, thus prompting an abrupt end to the post-election rally on 11 May, the very next trading day. The market then began a fall which continued through to the end of July.

As a general rule, slow-moving aspects between outer planets will not generally manifest in the market on the day they are exact, but only when they have been activated by a faster-moving planet. The Sun is a

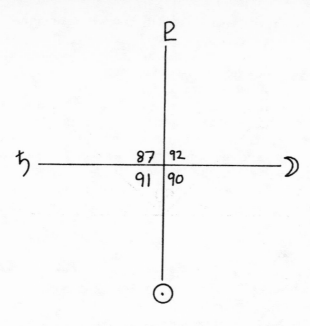

FIGURE 4.19

very important trigger for these aspects, as are Sun–Moon interactions that link into these patterns. The planet Mercury, which is astrologically associated with trading and commerce, can also act as an important trigger in the same way. Any slow-moving aspects between the outer planets that are not activated in this way will not pass unnoticed, but their effects will be more drawn-out and not as dramatic as when the aspects have been triggered. The triggering can, as we have seen with both the Jupiter–Saturn trines and the Saturn–Pluto squares, not just produce major moves, but also provide us with the exact date when the move begins!

The Saturn–Pluto squares of 1993–4 are interesting to examine, as unlike the first two examples we looked at, none of the squares in the sequence receive any close contacts from the Sun and Moon. The first instance of the square on 20 March did cause a 36-point fall in the FTSE Index on the first trading day after it was exact. The following weeks, however, did not see the continuing severe falls that usually follow a Saturn–Pluto square when it has been activated by the Sun and Moon. Instead, the market was marked by a general downward trend punctuated by brief rises. This provides a good illustration of the general rule that even when a Saturn–Pluto square has not been 'triggered', it is still a very potent negative factor as far as the market is concerned. An unactivated Saturn–Pluto square will generally tend to produce a continuing downward drift that can be periodically overridden and counteracted by other short-term cyclic and aspect effects.

The final Saturn–Pluto square of this sequence occurs at the beginning of 1994 and on 5 January is activated by the Sun and Moon.

Here we can again see a symmetric pattern forming at the time of a Sun–Moon square, with Pluto almost – but not quite – halfway between the Sun and Moon, and the Sun halfway between Saturn and Pluto. In addition, Mercury is also positioned very close to the Sun, adding to the pattern. This planetary picture is quite similar to that shown above for 4 January 1956 and we can expect a similar result, i.e., that the market should fall.

There are two additional planetary factors that should be noted for January 1994. In this instance, not only Mercury, but also Venus and Mars are very close to the Sun, and this will undoubtedly have the effect of strengthening the activation. The Sun and Moon do not, however, link into the Saturn–Pluto square quite as strongly as on previous occasions, when the triggering has produced strong falls. Further modifying and diminishing the effect of the square is the fact that the configuration will occur in January, a time when we would generally expect the market to rise, due to the effect of the Sun's annual cycle. January 1994 is not one of the key years when there would be a particularly strong rise, caused by the Sun's four-year cycle, but we would none the less generally expect to see the normal 'January rally'.

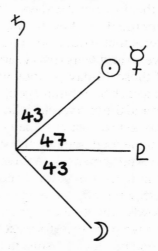

FIGURE 4.20

The astrological picture for January 1994 is complicated still further by the presence of the continuing Uranus–Neptune conjunction, which will be activated by Mercury, Venus and the Sun around this time, a factor that financial astrologers have suggested could cause a recovery. As the last time this conjunction occurred was in the 1820s, however, we have no hard financial data or evidence of its effects to draw on to form the basis for accurate predictions. We can make conjectures as to the likely effects of the conjunction, but the most sound and scientific course of action will simply be to wait and see what actually happens.

Taking all the various factors into consideration, however, we would expect the general trend to be down – not as strongly downward as might have been the case had these aspects occurred at a different point in the annual cycle, but downward nevertheless. All the astrological significators point to a strong possibility of economic recovery beginning in earnest shortly afterwards, so all in all, the first three weeks of January 1994 look set to be an extremely volatile time in the market.

ASPECTS TO THE SUN AND MARS

As well as considering the role of the Sun and other planets in relation to slow-moving cycles, Matlock also carried out research based on the Dow into the short-term effects of conjunctions and oppositions to the Sun and Mars. Different markets respond in different ways, so we felt it could be fruitful to extend his analysis to the UK and carried out our own research, which produced some extremely useful trading indicators.

Looking at the 14 calendar days – approximately 10 trading days – before and after the time of each conjunction and opposition allows us to identify effects that would otherwise be lost in the longer cycles of the Sun (one year) and Mars (two years). The following table shows the percentage of these 14-day periods when the market rose or fell. For example, taking each Sun–Jupiter conjunction, we look at the two weeks leading up to it and the two weeks following it, noting during each period whether the market rose or fell, then expressing the number of rises as a percentage of the total number of Sun–Jupiter conjunctions examined. Because of the long-term rising trend of the market, we would naturally expect to see more rises than falls, and over the period 1946–92, 57 per cent of the 14-day periods were up and 43 per cent were down. (Pluto moves very slowly, and its short-term aspects would give us little useful information, so we have therefore excluded Pluto from this study.) The Sun and Neptune produced results in line with chance; those that differ from chance are:

	Sun Conjunctions	
	14 days before % of times up	14 days after % of times up
Mars	—	73%
Jupiter	67%	—
Saturn	66%	—
Uranus	64%	—

	Sun Oppositions	
	14 days before % of times up	14 days after % of times up
Mars	45%	-
Uranus	—	69%

The strongest effect occurs after the Sun–Mars conjunction, where 73 per cent of the 14-day periods following it are up, but no significant effect can be observed before the conjunction. By contrast, the 14-day period preceding the Sun–Mars opposition produces a below average number of rises, especially if we recall that we would expect 57 per cent due to chance alone. Both Jupiter and Saturn show a small excess of rises before the solar conjunction but no effect afterwards and the oppositions show no effect at all. Uranus, however, shows an excess of rises after the opposition.

Looking at the effects of conjunctions and oppositions of Mars to the outer planets, we found the following particularly interesting results:

	Mars Conjunctions	
	14 days before % of times up	14 days after % of times up
Jupiter	—	19%
Uranus	50%	37%
Neptune	—	71%

	Mars Oppositions	
	14 days before % of times up	14 days after % of times up
Saturn	70%	65%
Uranus	63%	63%
Neptune	—	46%

The most striking result occurs after the Mars–Jupiter conjunction, when only 19 per cent of the following 14-day periods are up, and 81 per cent are down; the down periods vary in magnitude, but the preponderance of falls is very striking. Another weak period is that following the Mars–Uranus conjunction, when only 37 per cent are up, compared to the 57 per cent we would have expected by chance. The strong positive tone following the Mars–Neptune conjunction is also interesting, for as Uranus and Neptune are currently (1993) themselves conjunct, Mars hits both planets at the same time. Whereas Neptune tends to produce a rise after the Mars conjunction, Uranus generally yields a fall, so when Mars is conjunct both these planets simultaneously, the two effects may tend to cancel each other out.

Note that this is a possible indication for volatile markets – two factors working in opposite directions. The net effect may be to leave the market more or less where it is, but there can be strong up and down periods alternating with each other. On 29 January 1992 Mars came conjunct Uranus and on 1 February conjunct Neptune. The first two weeks of February showed a rise of 20 points on FTSE, then a fall of 50 points and finally a rise of 10 points – a small net move over the two weeks, but a 50-point range. Mars will again come conjunct both Uranus and Neptune from 16 January to 18 January 1994, and this is a further reason why we expect to see volatility in the last two weeks of January 1994.

In this chapter we have reviewed the main tools and techniques currently used by leading financial astrologers to predict market movements. In the following pages we will explore some further techniques that provide invaluable market cues – eclipses, retrogrades and charts for the actual times of market moves – as well as showing how these various techniques can be synthesised to create impressively accurate stock market forecasting models.

5

When is the Best Time to Buy and Sell?

For well over 150 years, ever since stock market speculation first became an established feature of business activity, acquiring foreknowledge of market moves has been the prime motivation of investors and market traders the world over. Until now, however, few speculators have known just how effective financial astrology can be in answering the question that is never far from their minds: when will the market move?

As we have seen, the astrology of the stock market involves studying many different factors and assessing how they will interact to produce either a bullish or a bearish trading influence at a particular time. Earlier, we looked at the major cycles, aspects and astrological 'triggers' that relate to the market, for these provide the basic structural information that underpins any change in direction, and are the starting-point for all forecasts and predictions. In this chapter we will see how the market predictions produced by combining cycles, aspects and triggers can be refined still further by considering some additional astrological phenomena – retrogrades, eclipses and the daily transiting angles. These additional factors can sometimes be the most important ones of all, for their presence in the astrological equation is often the final ingredient that kicks the market into a sudden dramatic rise or an equally sudden fall and can enable us to answer that all-important question: when is the best time to buy and sell?

Before looking at these additional factors in detail, it will be helpful to consider how the various tools and techniques featured in the preceding chapter can be combined to provide us with basic stock market predictions. The complexity of the world's stock markets in the late twentieth century means that any astrological analysis of the market will inevitably be correspondingly intricate. One of the best ways to understand how the various astrological cycles and aspects involved in the stock market unfold and work together in the hurly-burly of day-to-day trading is to explore how they were operating on two of the most famous occasions in market history, namely Black Monday in 1987 and the Wall Street Crash of 1929.

BLACK MONDAY: THE ASTROLOGICAL BACKGROUND

Mid-October 1987 was a period that some of the nation's leading financial astrologers predicted would spell trouble for the UK stock market many, many months in advance of the event. In a Chartsearch bulletin published in December 1986, Charles Harvey and Mike Harding gave their FTSE100 prediction for the upcoming year, which clearly showed the day of the crash and the subsequent market bottom on 11 November – although the actual magnitude of the fall exceeded even their gloomiest expectations. Exploring the picture in detail, we find, as we would expect, that many different astrological factors were working together to produce the crash. Factors which had bearish implications for world markets, not simply the UK alone.

From a cyclical perspective, the UK stock market on 19 October 1987 was in the falling phase of its annual solar cycle and the Sun–Mars double cycle, a powerful indicator in both the UK and US markets, was also moving downward. The short-term Moon–Jupiter single cycle was falling, and the double Moon–Jupiter cycle was at its peak and just beginning to turn down. Other cycles not hitherto explored in detail should also be mentioned, such as the Mars–Saturn cycle and the Venus–Uranus double cycle, as these were also in their falling phases and so also had a part to play in the crash. The cycles picture clearly indicates that the market was bearish, for most of the main cycles were falling or had hit their peaks and were beginning to turn down.

In addition, there were several important astrological triggers moving into place ready to activate the stock market on the 19th. The Sun was triggering the slow-moving Jupiter–Saturn trine on the day before (Sunday 18) by making an opposition to Jupiter, one of the classic astrological indicators for a market fall. In addition, Venus had entered Scorpio a week earlier, another negative factor, and Mercury, the planet of trading and commercial transactions, had come to a standstill – or 'stationed' – on the late afternoon of the previous Friday, a factor which, as we shall see shortly, often indicates that the existing market trend is about to alter.

Further storm-clouds were also gathering in the shape of certain aspects from transiting planets to the UK national chart and the UK Stock Exchange chart. Both these charts are important for assessing the market climate and transits to them can have considerable effects in terms of market moves. In the national chart transiting Saturn, the planet of restriction, was exactly conjunct the UK's Mercury (its trading power) on Black Monday, suggesting at the very least that there would be substantial difficulties and negative conditions in the trading markets. In addition, Uranus, the planet associated with sudden upsets and change, was trining the UK Saturn, thus giving a hint of the sudden and unexpected nature of the events that were about to unfold. It should be noted here that although transiting Saturn, which was affecting the UK Mercury, is traditionally associated with restriction and difficulty, Saturn in the natal chart of a country is generally interpreted as a symbol of its national sense of structure and stability. The transit of Uranus to the UK natal Saturn indicated, therefore, that some facet of the nation's stability was about to be violently overturned.

Strong destabilising factors were also showing up in the UK Stock Exchange chart. On 19 October Mars, the planet of energy and activation, was conjunct the Exchange's natal Uranus, and was also making difficult aspects to Venus and the Moon, thus suggesting the possibility of active trading and a strong, sudden move in the market. Finally, Neptune – a planet traditionally associated with confused happenings – was conjunct the Exchange's natal Moon, which symbolises its relationship with the public. Thus the aspect pattern (discussed in Chapter 1) involved with channelling financial resources from the investing public to the business community was being both energised by Mars – indicating active trading – and confused by Neptune. It would be hard to find a more apt description for the disorder of the day!

Considered from the standpoint of financial astrology, Black Monday provides a classic example of how many different factors can all come together at the same time to reinforce an essentially negative trend. The gloomy cycles picture was reinforced by several important triggers activating the long-term cycles that influence the market, thereby suggesting a fall. Further reinforcements of this trend were provided by transits to the UK national chart and Stock Exchange chart, thus providing not just one, but several indications for a market fall of considerable size.

We should emphasise that such a coincidence of factors homing in on one particular day is a very rare event, just as dramatic market moves (up or down) are similarly rare. But the astrologically aware investor, monitoring all the different factors, can anticipate such moves many months, or indeed years, in advance.

THE WALL STREET CRASH: A CONSPIRACY OF CYCLES

The US market crash of 1929 was a totally different animal from Black Monday. Whereas in 1987 the market had a severe fall but the downward plunge had burned itself out within a matter of days, the initial falls that took place in autumn 1929 were merely the beginning of the longest US stock market downturn in history. From the market peak at the beginning of September until the end of the first phase of the fall in mid-November, the market fell by 50 per cent. A brief respite followed, when speculators breathed again, mistakenly enjoying what history now calls the 'Sucker's Rally'. As shares regained approximately half their lost value, many investors thought it was safe to go back into the market, but in April 1930, the market resumed its downward slide with a vengeance. The day of 'The Crash' is singled out as 29 October because the falls starting on that day were so large and the air of panic so widespread. But it should be remembered that from 30 April 1930, when the 'Times Industrials' Index stood at 224, to July 1932, when it reached its lowest point of 58 (a fall of nearly 75 per cent), the market lost far more in value than during the crash itself. One of the best accounts of these events is contained in J. K. Galbraith's classic work *The Great Crash 1929*.

The astrology of the Wall Street Crash not only provides an interesting picture of how longer-term cycles can interact with shorter ones to produce major stock market downturns, but also illustrates the strikingly different ways in which the UK and US stock markets respond to the same cycles.

Experience has shown that the long-term cycles, such as Jupiter–Saturn, Jupiter–Uranus etc., exert a far stronger influence on stock market activity in New York than in London. In the UK, the long-term cycles are quite smooth, with a long gradual rise and a long-gradual fall, producing minimal effects on the market each day, week or even month. But in the US, these cycles are far more angular, which means they act very strongly indeed at certain points in the cycle. Thus they have the capacity to produce either steep rises or steep falls lasting for up to two or three years, with long periods in between these 'activation' times when their effect is quite small. This means that the longer-term cycles can produce much stronger moves in the US market than in the UK, and the main effects of the cycle – which incidentally also happen to be larger in the US than in the UK – are compressed into a timespan of 24–36 months, rather than the 10 years over which the cycle gently unfolds in the UK market.

As J. K. Galbraith wrote, looking back on the 1929 crash: 'There were no reasons for expecting disaster. No one could foresee that production, prices, incomes and all other indicators would continue to shrink through three long and dismal years.' No one that is, except those who were looking at the market from the perspective of the astrological cycles involved, such as W. D. Gann. As we have seen, he not only predicted the precise *day* the 1929 bull market would end, but also the three long years of misery that were to follow.

Assessing the activity of the long-term cycles in relation to short-term cycles also operating at the time allows us to see – as Gann did – not only why the US market crashed as it did, but also why it continued to fall for so long after the initial crash of 1929.

The crash itself was precipitated by several important shorter-term cycles, namely the Sun–Mars double cycle, the Mars–Saturn cycle and Mars–Pluto cycle, which were all coinciding in their falling phases in autumn 1929. A crucial cue for 29 October was also the Moon–Jupiter double cycle, which was turning downwards at that time.

But the main reason why the US market carried on falling was that not just one but several of the long-term cycles – which are the prime determinants of US stock market and economic activity – were all entering their sharp falling phases at the same time. This was the crucial factor which caused the stock market to continue its unrelenting downturn for so many months after the first fall. These long-term cycles were:

1. *Jupiter–Saturn* which peaked in August 1929 and fell until June 1932;
2. *Jupiter–Uranus* which peaked in September 1929 and fell until August 1932;
3. *Saturn–Pluto* which entered its falling phase in March 1930 and continued to fall until January 1933.

As we have seen, the Saturn–Pluto cycle is also important for the UK market, where the square aspects generally indicate a market fall. In the US, however, the really powerful falls are caused not by the squares, but by the opposition, and the time periods surrounding the formation of this hard aspect should always be watched carefully in New York. Although the Saturn–Pluto opposition was not directly involved in the Wall Street Crash, it was nevertheless a major contributor to the continuing falls of the early 1930s.

American readers will also be interested to note that the next opposition point in this cycle took place in 1966, when the US market fell by 20 per cent. Unlike the Saturn–Pluto opposition of the 1930s, this hard aspect was not reinforced by other difficult long-term cycles. This time around, there were favourable astrological influences at work which helped to neutralise the destructive power of the Saturn–Pluto opposition rather than reinforce it. Once again, we see how important it is to consider the whole astrological picture, not just one aspect or cycle alone. US readers may wish to note that the next Saturn–Pluto opposition occurs in 2001 and 2002.

COMBINING CYCLES TO PRODUCE TRADING INDICATORS

As the foregoing examples have demonstrated, the process of accurately forecasting stock market movements depends on our ability to identify and synthesise a considerable number of different cycles and astrological factors. When working with the economy, we can construct a model that will produce predictions for the timing of growth and recession using only four or five major cycles. But because the stock market responds to planetary influences on a day-by-day basis, obtaining precise timings for its movements requires far more information. Many more cycles, aspects and triggers must be taken into account. Generally speaking, the greater the number of astrological factors used to construct a working model of the stock market, the tighter and more accurate will be the predictions produced. But although it may on occasion be necessary to work with up to a dozen cycles at the same time, research has shown that reliable trading indicators can be derived by combining around half a dozen, or perhaps eight at the most, of the strongest stock market cycles.

The principle of combining cycles to produce trading indicators operates as follows. Any two cycles are constantly moving in and out of phase with each other, because of their different lengths. At certain times they will both be in a strongly rising phase; at others, they will both be falling. On the basis of the principles outlined above, we would expect to find that when two cycles reinforce each other in their rising phase, the resulting rise would be greater than for each cycle alone.

In order to show the effects of combining cycles, in the examples that follow we have quantified the resulting moves in terms of index points rather than percentage rises. This gives a value for the market move that is easier to understand. In these examples, we have assumed an index level of 3,000. In what follows, we will report the average effect over a number of occurrences of combining two or more cycles to produce a trading indicator. This does not mean that the indicator is infallible: sometimes the indicator has worked, sometimes not, but over a number of occurrences the net effect has been profitable.

For example, let's take two cycles which are known to produce strong effects in the UK stock market – the Sun–Mars single cycle and the Moon–Jupiter cycle – and see what happens when their rising phases coincide.

EXAMPLE 1

As we saw in Fig. 4.6, the strong rising phase of the Sun–Mars cycle takes place when the Sun is between 245 and 300 degrees ahead of Mars, when the market rises on average by about 13.6 points per week. Turning to the Moon–Jupiter cycle, as shown in Fig. 4.10, the strong rising phase of this short-term cycle occurs when the Moon is between 230 and 270 degrees ahead of Jupiter. Based on our standard index level of 3,000 points, this cycle considered in isolation tends to produce an average rise of around 19 index points per week.

If we confine ourselves to the period when both the Sun–Mars cycle and the Moon–Jupiter cycle are in their strongly rising phases and combine the two cycles, what we get is an average market rise of 29 points per week. We find, as we would have expected, that the average rise produced by combining these two cycles is greater than that produced by each cycle alone.

EXAMPLE 2

As a second example, let's stay with the Sun–Mars single cycle, but combine it with a different short-term lunar cycle, the Moon's 28-day cycle. As shown in Fig. 4.9, this cycle shows a strong rise between 225 and 270 degrees, and yields an average market rise of 11.4 points per week. The Sun–Mars cycle considered on its own produces rises of 13.6 points per week.

If we again confine ourselves to the period when both the Sun–Mars cycle and the Moon's 28-day cycle are in their strongly rising phases, we get a net average rise of 31.5 points per week.

We can see that using short-term factors like the Moon over a short range, as in the two examples given above, enables us to produce very short-term trading indicators and to identify a short time-span when we can predict that the market will rise. The lunar cycles are short-term and confining ourselves to the strongly rising phase only gives a 3–4 day period for the trading indication. In order to identify indicators operating over a longer period, it will be necessary to use longer-term cycles.

EXAMPLE 3

A longer-range indicator can be produced by combining two of the Mercury cycles discussed earlier. The Mercury–Uranus double cycle shown in Fig. 4.4 has a strong rising phase, as does the Mercury–Uranus single cycle between 50 and 180 degrees. If we take this rising phase of the single cycle when the double cycle is also rising, we get an average rise of 16 points per week. The heliocentric Mercury triple cycle (see Fig. 4.5) has a strong rising phase between 270 degrees of the first cycle and 90 degrees of the second cycle. Considered on its own, this produces average rises of 16 points per week.

When we combine these two Mercury cycles and focus on the times when both their rising phases coincide, we obtain an average rise of 39 points per weeks – a very strong rise indeed, compared to the effect produced by the single cycles alone.

Readers should note that as these two Mercury cycles can stay in phase for two, three or even four weeks at a time, the overall market rise produced by their interaction can average over 100 index points.

EXAMPLE 4

An impressive trading indicator can also be produced by combining the two Mercury cycles used in Example 3 with the Sun's four-year cycle, which is one of the strongest and most powerful cycles operating in the UK stock market. The strong rising phase of this cycle begins when the Sun enters Capricorn at the end of December in the first year and lasts until mid-Taurus in May of the second year. The average rise produced by this cycle alone is around 30.6 points per week over this dynamic four-and-a-half month period.

If we now combine the rising phase of the Sun's four-year cycle with those of the two Mercury cycles used above in a three-cycle test, the result is a staggering average rise of 96 points per week when all three cycles are rising simultaneously!

As more and more cycles are combined, the number of occasions when they are all in their rising phase falls. Even with the combination of just the four-year Solar cycle and the two Mercury cycles, we find just six occasions in the last 47 years when the cycles are all in phase. The more selective our combination, the less often it occurs – but the move that *does* occur will also be correspondingly stronger. By familiarising ourselves with the major cycles that produce effects in the stock market, how they interact and can be combined into trading indicators, and by knowing which cycles are in critical phases at any given time, we can anticipate and profit from these major moves.

It must be stressed that even with the help of the most sophisticated computer software, astrological analysis of the stock market is a highly complex process. Revolutionary new computer software which applies artificial intelligence to the complex web of stock market astrology is now in development in the UK and this will greatly aid market traders wishing to undertake the high-level cyclical analysis required to generate their own market forecasts. Meanwhile, the existing computer programmes such as 'Astro-Analyst', which enable traders to run several cycles simultaneously and assess their likely effects, are a good place to start. Readers should refer to the Directory of Resources for a full list of computer software.

Our account of the astrological cycles at work behind the scenes on Black Monday and during the Wall Street Crash showed how powerful the interaction of long and short-term cycles in the stock market can be, and the cyclical insights of astrology are undoubtedly impressive. But pinpointing precise market moves in advance is an extremely technical operation, and the specialised and time-consuming nature of this work means that it is presently still the exclusive province of a few highly skilled financial astrologers and market analysts – although the field is expanding all the time.

Readers should also remember that, in common with all other branches of forecasting, financial astrology is not a totally infallible guide to market activity, particularly when only a limited range of factors are taken into consideration. The full complement of astrological techniques is *always* required to produce an accurate stock market model, and though short-cuts are tempting, experience has shown that they are neither reliable nor rewarding.

NEW MOONS, FULL MOONS AND THE ANNUAL CYCLE

Another tried and tested approach to combining astrological factors to produce trading indicators is to use the cycle of New and Full Moons in conjunction with another strong UK cycle, such as the Sun's zodiac cycle. In our earlier discussion of astrological triggers, we saw that the Sun–Moon cycle does not in general behave like other cycles with their set patterns of rises and falls, but operates instead as one of the major catalysts or triggering mechanisms for bringing other cycles to life, such as the slow-moving Saturn–Pluto cycle. Research has shown that the monthly cycle of New and Full Moons interacts with the annual solar cycle, and can be used to obtain useful trading indications.

There are two periods each year when the UK stock market rises strongly: when the Sun is in Capricorn (December/January) and when it is in Aries (March/April). As the action of the Full and New Moons is different during both these two phases of the solar cycle and also quite complex, the easiest way of showing how it works is to divide the

Sun–Moon cycle into four equal parts, seven days before and after each New and Full Moon. As in the previous examples, the resulting average moves are shown in terms of points moved up or down based on a standard index of 3,000 points. First, we will look at what happens when the Sun is in Capricorn:

Sun in Capricorn

7 days before New Moon	+24 points
New Moon	
7 days after New Moon	+30 points
7 days before Full Moon	+24 points
Full Moon	
37 days after Full Moon	–3 points

Although the Sun in Capricorn is traditionally a 'strong rise' period, our results clearly show that there is one seven-day period when the market actually falls. This peculiarity can be used to formulate a useful trading rule. Before doing this, however, we need to look at what happens when the Sun is in Aries:

Sun in Aries

7 days before New Moon	+26 points
New Moon	
7 days after New Moon	+19 points
7 days before Full Moon	0 points
Full Moon	
7 days after Full Moon	+23 points

Again, we see that the traditional 'strong rise' period when the Sun is in Aries also has a weak spot, a seven-day period when the market does not exhibit its customary strength. When the Sun is in Capricorn, this weak period is the seven days *after* the Full Moon – when the Sun is in Aries, it is the seven days *before* the Full Moon. The effects of the Moon are modified by the Sun's position within its annual cycle.

A second way of looking at how the Sun–Moon cycle and annual cycle interact is to consider it in terms of 'strong moves', that is, by only looking at those seven-day periods when the market moves up or down by at least one per cent – or 30 points on our standard index of 3,000. If we calculate the percentage of these above-30-point moves that are up, we get the following:

Sun in Capricorn

7 days before New Moon	60%
New Moon	
7 days after New Moon	77%
7 days before Full Moon	76%
Full Moon	
7 days after Full Moon	59%

We can see that when the Sun is in Capricorn the period from New Moon to Full Moon has significantly more rises than the period from Full to New Moon.

Sun in Aries

7 days before New Moon	71%
New Moon	
7 days after New Moon	64%
7 days before Full Moon	52%
Full Moon	
7 days after Full Moon	81%

With the Sun in Aries, we see that the period from Full to New Moon (seven days after Full Moon and seven days before New Moon) has noticeably more rises than the New to Full Moon period. Indeed the seven days after the Full Moon are very strong indeed, with 81 per cent of large moves being up. What takes place when the Sun is in Capricorn is therefore the reverse of what happens when the Sun is in Aries. This shows quite clearly that the two cycles are actually interacting, rather than simply adding their effects together. This interaction does not show up with the Sun in other signs.

When we considered planetary cycles, particularly in relation to the economy, we were able to produce a good predictive model by adding together the results from a number of cycles. Here we cannot do that. The results show why the Sun–Moon cycle *seems* to have little effect on the UK market when considered as a cycle. The effect of the same phase of the cycle can be not just different, but opposite, depending on the Sun's position in its annual cycle.

We can now formulate a trading rule based on the results of this behaviour. If you are thinking of buying when the Sun is in Capricorn, it's best to do so at the New Moon, which is the start of the strong period. If you wish to sell when the Sun is in Capricorn, do it at the Full Moon, straight after the strong rise and just before the weakest seven-day period.

If you want to buy when the Sun is in Aries, do so at the Full Moon, just after the 'weak' seven-day period and at the start of the strongest two weeks. But if you are selling when the Sun is in Aries, do so at the New Moon, just as the strong period draws to a close.

Readers should note that these results are based on research into the UK stock market and it should not be assumed that they will work for other markets. A similar analysis carried out for those markets would probably yield quite different findings. Remember too that these are *average* results, based on how these two cycles have interacted over a number of years. Sometimes this trading indicator will work, sometimes it won't – but working with these cycles and noting how they interact with each other will definitely put the odds in your favour.

RETROGRADES AND PLANETARY STATIONS: CHANGING MARKET TRENDS

We will now turn our attention to the specific 'fine-tuning' techniques that can be used to pinpoint those all-important days when the market is most likely to turn.

First, we shall look at the influence that retrograde planets can have on the stock market. As we saw earlier, when viewed from the Earth (geocentrically), Mercury and Venus cannot form normal cycles either with each other or with the Sun because they are always so close to the Sun – although they do have heliocentric cycles. But although we cannot treat their geocentric cycles with each other or with the Sun in the same way as the other planets, Mercury and Venus can nevertheless provide us with useful information. As Mercury and Venus move around the Sun, and the Earth moves in relation to them, there are certain times when they appear to move backwards – or retrograde – as we explained in Chapter 1. These alternating times of direct and retrograde motion have been found to produce a market effect.

The most common occurrence is for both planets to be direct. During this time, no deviation from the general market trend can be observed. If one or both planet is retrograde, however, a small effect is found:

Mercury	Venus	Stock Market Effect
Direct	Direct	Nil
Retrograde	Direct	Slightly Down
Direct	Retrograde	Up
Retrograde	Retrograde	Down

The strongest effects occur when Venus is retrograde. If Mercury is also retrograde at the same time, the market displays a small but significant tendency to fall. If Mercury is direct at the same time, the reverse happens and the market tends to rise. These effects are not powerful in themselves, but they are worth watching, for they do provide a general bullish or bearish background trend. When Venus is retrograde at an important event, such as an eclipse, the up or down tendency (depending on Mercury) is accentuated and becomes locked in for a period.

The stations of Venus and Mercury (when the motion changes from direct to retrograde or from retrograde to direct) are important, as they mark jumps from one background trend to another. So if Venus were retrograde and Mercury stationed from retrograde to direct motion, there would be a switch from a down to an up trend. Or, if Venus changed from direct to retrograde while Mercury was retrograde, there would be a change from a slightly down trend to a more strongly down trend.

On 16 October 1987, the Friday before the crash of Black Monday, Mercury stationed prior to going retrograde, thus suggesting a switch to a downward market trend. On a more positive note, observers ascribed the market upturn on 9 April 1992 to the Conservative election victory, but it is worth noting that Mercury also stationed before turning direct on the same day – thereby confirming that the prevalent trend would change to an upward one.

While the stations of Mercury are consistent – a change from direct to retrograde has a negative effect in the market and the change from retrograde to direct is positive – Venus stations can work in either direction, depending on whether Mercury is itself direct or retrograde. For example, on 23 May 1988, Venus stationed before going retrograde with Mercury direct, indicating a change of trend from neutral to up, and this station did in fact mark the start of a rally in the market. The Venus station to retrograde on 11 March 1993 took place when Mercury was also retrograde and here the slight downward trend changed into a much steeper fall. (Readers should note how this reinforced the Mercury heliocentric cycle already mentioned in relation to the March UK market high.)

The Venus effect is determined by Mercury's motion. If Mercury is direct when Venus stations before going retrograde, the background trend changes from neutral to up. But if Mercury is retrograde and Venus then also turns retrograde, the trend switches from slightly down to more strongly down. The fact that Venus has stationed cannot provide the basis for a trading decision without taking into account the action of Mercury. The stations of Mercury and Venus are always worth noting, as they frequently mark a change of trend in the market. As we discussed in Chapter 4, long-term cycles require a trigger before they become active. The stations of Mercury and Venus can often provide that trigger.

THE POWER OF ECLIPSES

One of the most important timing mechanisms for identifying market moves is the eclipse, which for centuries has enjoyed a distinctly dubious reputation in astrological and non-astrological circles alike. In fact, the bad public image of eclipses is not totally justified, since eclipses can usher in sudden upturns as well as falls, but if we cast our imagination back for a moment to prehistoric times, it's easy to see how the fear and foreboding that have long surrounded this celestial phenomenon came into being.

To early man, the planets were literally gods and within the framework of his limited, unscientific understanding, dramatic events in the skies were thought to portend equally dramatic events on Earth. Imagine for instance the terror that must have arisen when a total eclipse of the Sun took place and day turned to night as the Sun totally disappeared ... or the panic he felt at seeing a lunar eclipse, when a strange dark shadow seemed to engulf the Full Moon and extinguish its light from the sky without warning. Eclipses were considered to be the messengers of death, doom and disaster, and thus acquired a bad press in early astrology – a tendency which has lingered on to the present day.

Considered from the purely practical standpoint of financial astrology, however, eclipses are essentially another form of astrological trigger, and produce negligible effects by and of themselves. Their 'difficult' reputation has arisen because they can indeed act very powerfully – but only if they coincide with some other group of astrological factors which they can lock into and activate. If no strong patterns are present in the astrology of the moment, the eclipse will pass almost unnoticed. If there *are* other powerful factors present, however, the eclipse will function as a kind of amplifier and bring the whole market dynamic to life. When eclipses happen at such times, the effects in the market can be devastating or astounding – or even both – as we shall see ...

In basic astronomical terms, solar eclipses occur when the Moon comes between the Earth and the Sun, and therefore only take place at New Moons. Lunar eclipses, on the other hand, happen when the Earth comes between the Sun and the Moon, and the shadow cast by the Earth falls onto the Moon, and thus only occur at Full Moons. Eclipses do not take place on every New or Full Moon, however, since a further astronomical condition must also be fulfilled: that the Sun, Moon and Earth are all in a straight line. For this to take place, the Moon must be within 18 degrees of its North or South Node – if it is positioned further away than this, no eclipse will occur.

The number of solar eclipses varies each year, but there are always at least two, which take place roughly six months apart. Although solar eclipses are therefore relatively common, they are actually only visible within a very limited surface area of the earth, which is known as the 'eclipse path'. Lunar eclipses generally occur two or three times a year, within a fortnight or so of a solar eclipse, and are for the most part far more generally visible.

For a total eclipse of the Sun to be visible in a particular location is indeed a rare event and even with our superior understanding, we can see why the ancients considered it such an impressive event. For forecasting purposes, however, all eclipses should be considered, even invisible ones!

From the perspective of cyclical analysis, eclipses are significant because they represent the interaction of two important cycles: the Sun–Moon cycle, whose role as a key trigger mechanism has already been discussed at length, and the Moon's Node cycle. In order for eclipses to take place at all, these two cycles must be aligned. At solar eclipses, the Sun is conjunct the Moon and at lunar eclipses, the Sun is opposing the Moon. Both these aspect patterns must also conjoin either the North or South Node: the nodal cycle is therefore also at a critical point. Finally, we should also check to see exactly where the action takes place in the yearly zodiac cycle, for if, as sometimes happens, a critical seasonal point is triggered, such as 0 degrees Aries – then a third cyclical factor will be brought into play by the eclipse, making it even more powerful as a trigger for events.

Eclipses (1): Triggering Global Falls

A striking example that shows how eclipses can function as extremely powerful triggers for stock market moves occurred on 6 August 1990, when a lunar eclipse took place shortly after 3 p.m. BST. Eclipses exert their strongest effects when they lock into a powerful aspect pattern or planetary configuration that is already present and this is precisely what happened on the day in question. The activation of a major planetary pattern was instantaneous and far-reaching, producing dramatic falls world-wide which were particularly severe in New York. A closer examination of the full astrological background to the eclipse tells us why ...

The Sun–Moon opposition formed at 90 degrees to a Mars–Pluto opposition, creating the difficult planetary configuration known in astrology

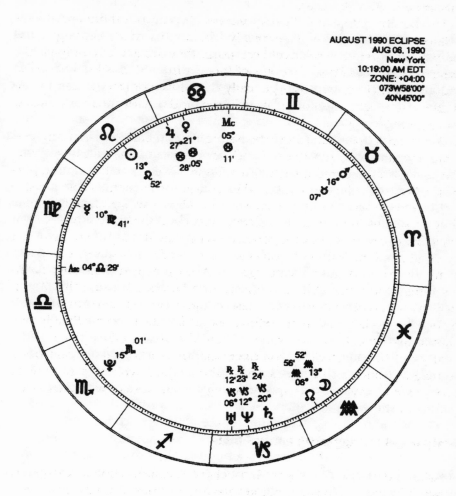

FIGURE 5.1: 6 AUGUST 1990 ECLIPSE

as a 'Grand Cross'. Pluto can be an extremely destructive planet for the stock market, and in this instance its effect was being amplified and energised by a hard aspect to Mars. The presence of this difficult aspect alone would have been sufficient to indicate trouble for the market. The additional involvement of a lunar eclipse, an extremely powerful trigger, added fuel to the fire and provided a further warning that the fall would be severe. Added to this was the fact that Pluto was in Scorpio, another key placement for the market. All four planets involved in the Grand Cross were therefore in the fixed signs – Taurus, Leo, Scorpio and Aquarius – which is often a significant position for the markets. When strong planetary patterns such as a Grand Cross fall in these areas of the zodiac, it is always a cue to watch the market carefully at that time. As well as the eclipse and the Grand Cross in fixed signs, Venus, the planet of money, was opposing Saturn, the planet of restriction, adding yet another gloomy note to the proceedings – not one, but many cues from the cosmos that 6 August would be a day to remember in the markets.

As the eclipse formed, the UK market started to fall and as the Moon moved to oppose the Sun exactly, the fall became a collapse. As the eclipse reached its maximum at 3.13 p.m. (shortly before the exact opposition), the UK market was down 60 points, but from this point onwards, when the eclipse had passed the point of maximum intensity, the market suddenly stopped falling. A minor rally then ensued and the market recovered to some degree, but after a further, more controlled fall, it still finished 64 points down on the day.

Since an eclipse is a global phenomenon, other world markets were similarly affected, particularly New York. The New York Stock Exchange was open and trading at the time of the eclipse, and the market began to fall around the same time as it did in London. As the falls continued, panic broke out, and the city's telephone and computer lines began to hum with all kinds of wild rumours. In New York too, the worst moment of the day came when the eclipse reached its maximum. At that precise moment, the Dow-Jones was off 160 points, a fall that had been accomplished in little more than half an hour. As the eclipse subsided, the market began to recover, but just as in London, it still finished well down on the day.

Why was the fall so much more severe in New York? To answer this question, we must look to the US Stock Exchange chart, which was being closely triggered by the hostile planetary alignments of the day. In the US Exchange chart, Uranus, the planet of sudden and unexpected events, lies at 15 degrees of Leo, which meant that it exactly squared transiting

Pluto and was linking straight in to the destructive energy of the eclipse. In addition, at the very height of the eclipse, transiting Uranus was conjunct the transiting IC in New York. This highlighted the Uranus and further emphasised the sudden and extreme nature of the collapse. No such powerful links were to be found to the transiting angles in the UK or to the UK Exchange chart, with the result that falls in New York were markedly more severe than in the UK.

To summarise the day's events, a very negative Mars–Pluto opposition formed a major pattern, the Grand Cross, with the eclipsed Full Moon. All four planets were in a powerful position in the middle of the fixed signs and in New York they also linked into the Uranus of the Stock Exchange chart, thus suggesting sudden disruption. In addition, transiting Uranus was further emphasised by being placed exactly on a chart angle (the IC) in New York. And just for good measure, Saturn, the planet of restriction, was opposing Venus, the planet of money. Once again, we see not just one, but many different factors all coming together at the time of a major market move.

Eclipses (2): Prologue to Black Monday

The days following the eclipse of 7 October 1987 provide a good example of how an eclipse can lock in to a planetary configuration and release its effects over a longer period of time – in this case, the events that were seen in the world's stock markets on Black Monday, some 12 days later. The contacts made by the eclipse in both London and New York also explain why the subsequent patterns of trading in both countries assumed such radically different styles in the calamitous days that followed.

When the eclipse of 7 October occurred, Mercury, the planet of trading, was conjunct Pluto, the planet of power and destruction, thus providing an early warning of the troubled trading to come. Two other factors that were present at this eclipse, which was of course a global event, should also be noted. First, in London at the time of the eclipse, Saturn was exactly angular on the IC, thus strongly emphasising this planet of restriction. While in New York, it was Mars that fell on the IC, which meant that it was this energising planet that was emphasised. Mars was thus locked in in New York and Saturn in London, creating a pattern that 12 days later led to a very strong fall in both markets. Note that in New York, where the dynamic energy of Mars was angular at the eclipse, the crash occurred in one day; whereas in London, where restrictive and delaying Saturn was angular, the crash took place initially over two days, with the falls continuing thereafter.

The eclipse of 7 October 1987 also linked in to the UK national chart, falling exactly on the nodal axis. In financial astrology, the North and South Nodes symbolise associations of people, thus suggesting that the eclipse would affect many people – which, of course, it did. The US national chart was also activated by the eclipse, with the Sun conjunct the US Saturn and the Moon opposing it, thus suggesting that conditions of pessimism and restriction were likely to follow. Thus we can see that the October eclipse prepared the ground for Black Monday, by locking in a finely meshed web of astrological factors in the run-up to the subsequent global crash.

Eclipses (3): Sparking A Rise

Happily, eclipses do not always spell bad news for the market; their presence can signal a sudden rise as well as a fall. One occasion on which this positive triggering effect was particularly strongly marked was 21 December 1991, when an eclipse took place at 10.23 a.m. GMT. This time, the effects of the eclipse were not felt simply on the stock exchanges of London and New York, but on many other markets round the world, including commodity markets, which all turned in response to this eclipse.

What made this eclipse so powerful was its position on one of the four main cardinal or seasonal points, for it occurred just as the Sun was about to enter Capricorn. As we have seen, this point in the solar cycle is usually the cue for the New Year rally. These cyclical factors alone would have sparked an upturn and, in the event, the eclipse acted as the trigger for a sudden rise. In addition, the expansive planet Jupiter was trine Uranus, an aspect which generally produces a very positive effect on the market. Further bullish factors were provided by the positioning of Venus, the planet of money, halfway between the Jupiter–Uranus trine and also by the fact that Mercury, the planet of trading, was falling exactly on the Midheaven in London at the time of the eclipse, which duly served to amplify its effect on the markets.

The only note of uncertainty was introduced by the fact that Venus, whilst making its favourable contacts with Jupiter and Uranus, was also conjunct Neptune, the planet of confusion, in the UK national chart and squaring the UK natal Venus. The link to Neptune endowed the rise with a panicky character, as though traders feared they might miss the boat. The square to Venus underlined the eclipse's relation to the financial markets and gave the clearest possible signal that this particular eclipse was bound to spark substantial market moves.

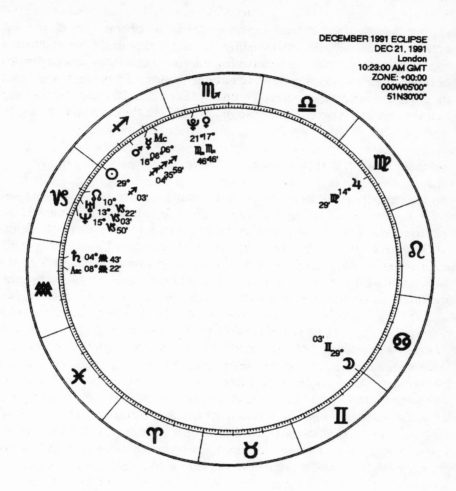

FIGURE 5.2: 21 DECEMBER 1991 ECLIPSE

THE ANGLES: THE ART OF TIMING MAJOR MARKET MOVES

Like eclipses and Sun–Moon aspects, the angles of the daily chart can act as important triggers for transiting planetary patterns. For those who are seeking to time their market activity to the exact hour of the day, it is no overstatement to say the angles are the most crucial factor to consider, for it is angular contacts alone that have the capacity to indicate the exact *time* of day that a market move is likely to take place. As such vital information is so hard, if not impossible, to determine by more conventional means, these astrological techniques are now beginning to find more widespread application in the financial markets of the world. Many of the intra day traders of the Chicago financial futures pits use financial astrology widely in their trading and their main timing tool is the action of the transiting angles in triggering the planetary configurations occurring that day. Just as with eclipses, however, the triggering mechanism of the angles can only operate if there is a pattern lying dormant in the astrological make-up of the day waiting to be triggered off. But when the conditions are right, the effect of the angles can be extremely powerful, as the following examples show.

EXAMPLE 1

Our first example took place in the US stock market. On 20 October 1988, the pattern shown in Fig. 5.3 formed during the last hour of trading on the New York Exchange.

Saturn and Uranus are conjunct, and this aspect is being squared by the energetic energy of Mars. At the same time, the Sun and Moon are 120 degrees apart, thus forming a trine; in addition, and most importantly, Uranus was positioned exactly midway between the Sun and Moon. The angles provide the timing mechanism because planets conjunct the transiting angles are highlighted and operate very powerfully. In this case, the angles triggered the existing configuration when the Midheaven hit the Saturn–Uranus conjunction and the Ascendant came conjunct Mars at the same time. The results were dramatic. Having been flat for most of the day, the New York market suddenly rose 45 points in the last hour of trading!

Just as in the many other examples of triggering already discussed, the market move in Example 1 was caused by a symmetric pattern locking in several astrological factors at a certain point in time. The likelihood of a short-term rise in the market was implicit in the planetary

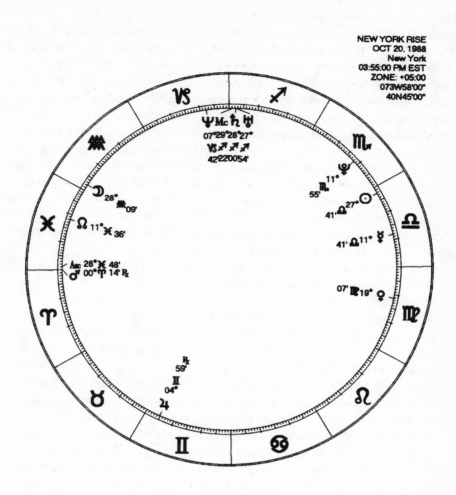

FIGURE 5.3: 20 OCTOBER 1988

geometry of the days both before and after 20 October, for Mars was
square Uranus, thus indicating the potential for a sudden release of activity for a number of days. Before this could take place, however, the
Sun–Moon trine had to form and Uranus take up its position midway
between the Sun and Moon so that the dynamic energy of the
Mars–Uranus square could be released when they contacted the angles.
The market thus move depended on the angular contact triggering not
just one, but several different factors.

   Earlier in the day, no major leap occurred in the London market when
the angles contacted the Mars–Uranus square and it is instructive to ask
why. Basically, five hours earlier, the Sun–Moon trine had not yet quite
formed. In addition, the point midway the Sun and Moon was not so
close to Uranus, being over a degree away, compared to the close contact of one-sixtieth of a degree that existed at the time the angles triggered the pattern in New York. When the angles in London came to the
same relative position with Uranus on the Midheaven and Mars on the
Ascendant, no market move took place because there was no exact interlocking pattern to trigger.

EXAMPLE 2

Our second example is also based on events in the New York stock
market, but also has interesting predictive implications for London.
On 16 August 1991, Wall Street suddenly fell 40 points in a mere
half-hour, from about 12.45 to 1.15 p.m. New York time. From the
ephemeris we can see that on that afternoon there was a conjunction of the Moon and Pluto. Looking at the chart for the time of the
conjunction, we see that it fell within three degrees of the Ascendant
in New York. Pluto, as we have seen, can be a very destructive planet
for the stock market and so its conjunction with the Moon must be
important. But this conjunction takes place every month and the
New York market doesn't tumble dramatically in this manner every
month, so what are the other vital factors that caused the fall?

   First, and most important, the Moon–Pluto conjunction was emphasised by being placed so close to the Ascendant. A second factor was
that the conjunction occurred exactly halfway between Mars and
Neptune. Although these planets were not in a traditional aspect, the
symmetrical pattern thus formed was very powerful. Again, it was the
energy of Mars that we have seen in action before, this time added to
the confusing, panic-prone influence of Neptune. Finally, both Mercury
and Venus were retrograde, and although this was not a major factor, it

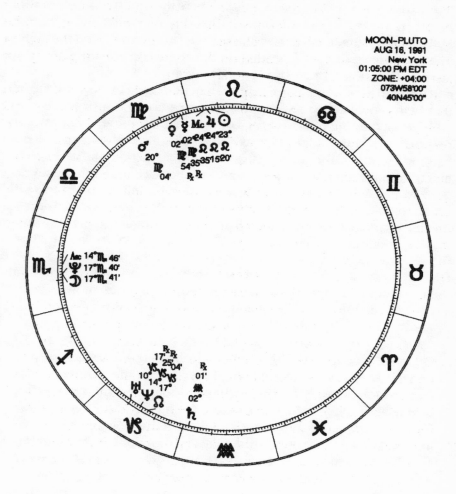

FIGURE 5.4: MOON–PLUTO CONJUNCTION; 16 AUGUST 1991

nevertheless added weight to the strongly negative conjunction of the Moon and Pluto on the Ascendant.

Incidentally, the conjunction took place at 17 degrees of Scorpio and, as we have seen, Scorpio is a position where the Moon can show a slight rise and trigger bullish indicators. In this case, however, there were no bullish indicators to trigger and as the Moon's conjunction with Pluto was intrinsically bearish, on this occasion the Moon's transit through Scorpio was not marked by a rise. The coincidence of a Moon–Pluto conjunction happening during the trading hours of a market and in addition being so close to the Ascendant is quite rare.

If we look at the effect on the London market of these conjunctions on their own without considering the angles, we find they produce no marked results. But if we stipulate the further condition that the conjunctions must fall within five degrees of the Ascendant, then an effect does emerge. In fact, on every occasion that a conjunction of this kind has taken place since 1947, the market has fallen. Since the market has fallen every single time this happens, we can form a trading rule based on this principle. N.B. In the New York example we looked at above, the fall was quite strong and this was due to the added effect of the Mars–Neptune symmetric pattern, which will not be present every time the conjunction occurs. In addition, the effect is much more powerful if the conjunction occurs during market hours.

EXAMPLE 3

Our final example looks at how the transiting angles triggered a move in the London market. On 28 April 1993, the following configuration occurred. Mercury was square the prevailing Uranus–Neptune conjunction, thus creating the perfect conditions for busy but confused trading. In addition, the Moon was opposing the conjunction, thus introducing an emotional, somewhat irrational air to the proceedings. Saturn was square Pluto, but the aspect was inexact and therefore needing triggering before its presence could be strongly felt. The necessary trigger was provided by the Moon, which trined Pluto, and the market was finally pushed into action by the angular contact of Saturn on the Descendant, an angular contact which exactly marked the low point of the day.

The temporary strengthening of Saturn (by being angular) and Pluto (by being trine the Moon) activated the Saturn–Pluto square, in much the same way as the Sun–Moon triggers we looked at in Chapter 4. The market fell to the exact time that Saturn was angular and then began to recover.

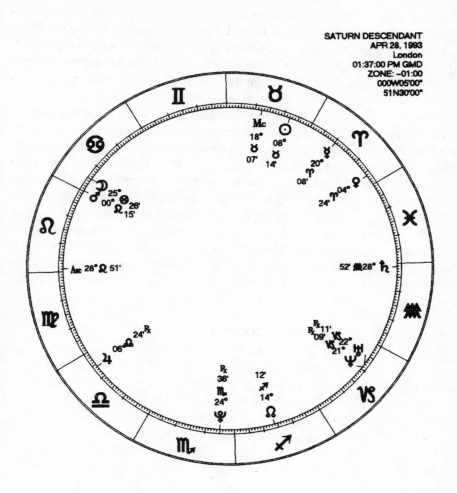

FIGURE 5.5: SATURN CONJUNCT DESCENDANT; 28 APRIL 1993

As a general principle, angular transits like those described above occur four times each day, as the four angles move through the full circle of the zodiac. In the above example, the activating effect of the Moon–Pluto trine provided a window of a few short hours during which the potential existed for the Saturn–Pluto square to be activated by an angle. Such angular transits are not sufficiently powerful to trigger market moves in themselves, but when they contact strong planetary patterns, the resulting market effects can be extremely pronounced.

As we have seen, there are many different factors that affect stock markets and the greatest challenge facing any potential investor is knowing which tools and techniques to incorporate into a market model that will be suited to his or her particular trading needs. Very many different factors affect the market and in our discussion we have endeavoured to introduce those that we feel are most important. But we must emphasise that this is only an introduction to this highly complex field.

Readers should note that these techniques are also applicable to other markets, such as exchange rates, interest rates and of course commodities – although using these tools in different markets will of course yield different results.

How Astrology Can Help your Company

While the economic downturn of recent years has curtailed growth in many sectors of business and finance, the manifest failure of orthodox economics to detect the onset of recession has paradoxically ushered in a new wave of interest in less conventional forms of forecasting such as financial astrology. Those in business who might hitherto have dismissed the idea of using astrology are now turning to it in increasing numbers, as the practical benefits to companies and institutions of using this highly flexible forecasting approach become more widely proven and accepted in financial circles.

In many countries in the Orient, particularly Hong Kong and India, astrology has been in continuous use as a forecasting and business tool from ancient times up to the present day, but it is only in comparatively recent years that entrepreneurs and financial analysts in the West have acquired any understanding of its value. In America, particularly on the West Coast and in New York, but increasingly also in Europe and the UK, many business people are now discovering to their advantage that astrology can be used not only to predict the economy and the stock market, but also to guide forward planning and investment at the grass-roots level of their own companies. Astrologers who specialise in business advice on both sides of the Atlantic have all reported a growing interest in their work from the business community and it is expected that this valuable 'new wave' business practice will gain ever-increasing ground as the decade proceeds.

So what are the specific advantages that using astrological insights can offer your company? The benefits cover the whole spectrum of business activity and fall broadly into the following categories:

1. First and most importantly, astrology can provide a picture of the future trading prospects for the company and indicate the best times for business expansion – as well as times when it will be more prudent to retrench and consolidate.
2. What are the danger periods for finance? When will cash flow be strong? When will it be problematic?
3. When is the best time to take on extra debt? And when would it be better to avoid this?

4. How can you assess the public perception of your company?
   When will your company be seen in a favourable light and
   when will you need to put extra effort into promoting your
   public image?
5. What can astrology reveal about the implications of all the
   above factors for the share price of your company?

The most important advantage that financial astrology brings to company management is that, correctly used, it enables forecasts to be made
about the timing of likely developments within the business with a degree
of precision and confidence; something no other technique can provide.
Just as the economy and the stock market can be affected favourably or
unfavourably by astrological cycles and aspects, companies too are also
subject to such rhythms. These cyclical fluctuations are the root cause
of each company's 'good times' and 'bad times', and becoming familiar
with the underlying cyclical factors that are affecting the business allows
the right decisions to be made at the right time, so that the company
can swim with the tides of commerce, rather than struggle against them.
For as business managers know only too well, choosing the right *time*
to expand or change the direction of the company is the most important task they face. Using basic company astrology will allow managers
to improve their business timing significantly and so help their company
to always stay one step ahead of the competition.

COMPANY ASTROLOGY: TOOLS AND TECHNIQUES

1. The Company Birthchart

The starting-point for the astrology of a particular company is its birthchart.
Like the national and stock exchange charts we looked at earlier, the
company chart is based on the date, time and place that the company
came into existence. For a UK company, the 'date of birth' is the day on
which the company was incorporated by the Registrar of Companies.
Due to a quirk of British law, the company exists for the whole of the
day on which the official incorporation takes effect, so the time at which
the company came into being is always midnight at the start of that day.
All UK company charts are therefore set up for midnight GMT – or midnight BST if they are incorporated during summer time. The company's
'place of birth' also needs to be specified; it is normal practice to use

the location of the company's head office. In certain cases – for example, when the company has undergone a merger or changed its name and image radically – it may be more appropriate to use the birthchart for the 'new' company, rather than its original incorporation date. This idea will be explained in more detail when we look at the history of the retail group Next.

Interpreting the company's birthchart allows us to assess its strengths and weaknesses, as well as to pinpoint times when the business is likely to prosper or suffer difficulties. In order to fully understand how a company birthchart works, it will be useful at this point to expand on the planetary meanings we introduced in Chapter 1.

2. The Planets

In analysing company charts, we need to first consider the meanings of the planets in the birthchart, also known as their natal positions. These natal positions tell us all we need to know about the company's basic structure – or what it was 'born' with, its inherent strengths and weaknesses. Being aware of the company's innate weak points is just as important as knowing the strengths that can be built on and developed.

As the planets are constantly moving in the heavens, the company's natal planets are continually being aspected by planetary transits. So we also need to look at what the planets signify by transit, as this provides key insights into what is happening to the company at any time. For instance, a company's management is likely to take a very different view of things when it is enjoying a favourable Jupiter transit to its Sun, as opposed to when it is battling to survive under difficult transits of Saturn or Pluto. Becoming familiar with transits allows us to take full advantage of times of opportunity, as well as to 'batten down the hatches' when tough times loom ahead.

In financial astrology, the planets in the birthchart – and by transit – have the following meanings:

The Sun

The Sun symbolises the company itself, its essential life force and drive. It also stands for the company's founder, the owner of the business and the top management. The Sun also represents government and authority figures.

By transit, the Sun focuses attention on whatever part of the chart it is moving through. The annual transit of the Sun over the Midheaven – the area of the chart that describes the company's business objectives – may mean that corporate goals will be re-evaluated at this time. If the natal Sun is hit by an eclipse, it will bring about major changes in the direction of the business or indicate a change at the top. Eclipses can also lock in whatever transits are occurring at the time and trigger any planetary aspects occurring at the time.

The Moon

The Moon in the company birthchart describes the public image of the company, and how the public reacts to the company's products and services. Also, it signifies the people who buy the products – the company's customers and the mass markets. The Moon also symbolises the company's employees. A badly-aspected natal Moon may indicate a poor public image. Hard aspects from Saturn, Neptune or Pluto can point to problems with employees. On a mundane level, the Moon is associated with agriculture and products for the mass market.

Mercury

Mercury is one of the key financial planets for any business, as it symbolises trade, transactions, dealing and selling of all kinds. The natal position of Mercury in the company chart reveals much about the sales, service and communication capacities of the business, as well as ideas, business plans and the capacity for travel. Companies with a strong natal Mercury are frequently found in the publishing, travel, news media and postal service sectors. Natally, Mercury also describes the commercial, analytical and scientific abilities of the people in the business, as well as what the company's relationship with the media is likely to be. Difficult aspects to natal Mercury can indicate problems in selling the company's products and trading difficulties in general.

By transit, Mercury can bring news about the company and is usually prominent when mergers, company acquisitions or other important developments are *announced*. When transiting Mercury turns retrograde, a company may run into problems and experience delays with communication and trading.

Venus

In the natal chart, Venus stands for a company's resources, its assets and its money. It is particularly important in assessing cash flow. It also tells us how popular the company is with the public and whether its products are likely to find favour. A well-placed Venus is often found in the charts of companies in the fashion, music, beauty and leisure industries. Like Mercury, Venus is a key financial planet for a company: a retrograde Venus is not a helpful position in a company chart, as it indicates problems with financial resources and money. It should, if possible, be avoided by choosing an alternative incorporation date.

By transit, Venus can make the company's products more popular with the public and investors, and can also bring about financial developments in a business.

Mars

Natal Mars stands for the motivation, drive and energy of a business, its competitive spirit, individual identity and ability to act. Mars is also associated with the military sector, munitions, sport, machinery, equipment and the ability to make things (manufacturing).

By transit, Mars brings activity and is an important trigger of action. When Mars turns retrograde, the drive of the business can diminish, thereby reducing the level of activity.

Jupiter

A key business planet, natal Jupiter indicates a company's potential to grow and be successful, the ability to generate profits and the financial resources represented by Venus. Jupiter is also the chief indicator of expansion. Jupiter can indicate a company's links with banking, broking, legal matters and public relations, as well as its involvement with foreign concerns and education.

By transit, Jupiter signifies good times for business, and is the primary symbol of expansion and prosperity. Growth and expansion are not always good, however. Difficult Jupiter transits can incline a company to overexpand beyond its resources or to be overconfident in its abilities.

Saturn

Another key business planet, natal Saturn describes the company's internal structures and its administrative and management abilities. A weak Saturn can indicate problems with or a lack of internal structures. Saturn also reveals the ability to consolidate, take stock and bring things down to earth, and administrative and management abilities. It also stands for that part of the company where responsibility lies – the board of directors. A strong Saturn suggests the company will be conservative and traditional in its attitudes. Business activities associated with Saturn include property, farming, mining, products for the elderly and 'traditional' products.

Difficult Saturn transits, such as squares and oppositions, bring restrictions and financial problems, and cause unexpected delays in business development. A natal planet contacted by transiting Saturn will experience restriction and difficulties in the area of company activity it represents.

Uranus

Natal Uranus indicates the company's ability to be innovative, progressive and to produce new ideas and inventions. It also gives it the desire to stand out from the crowd, and be seen as somehow different and original in its approach. Uranian companies are future-orientated and are often involved with electronics, computers, radio, high-tech developments, airlines or any products at the forefront of technology.

Positive transits of Uranus can herald the announcement of an exciting new invention or the company may radically depart from the conventional way of doing things. Uranus transits can also indicate company breakups, sudden expansion, or a sudden change in direction or the fortunes of the business. Sudden and unexpected events and changes are the usual hallmarks of Uranus transits.

Neptune

Natally, Neptune stands for the company's image, its ideals, dreams and its vision. Negatively, it indicates the capacity for self-delusion, confusion and unwillingness to face reality. On the positive side, it stands for inspiration and altruism. Neptune is associated with the advertising industry, cinema and television, the arts, hospitals and healing, drugs and chemicals, the wine and the brewing trade, oil and shipping. It is also connected with poisons and toxic wastes.

Hard Neptune transits can bring business problems stemming from rumours, scandal-mongering or imprudent developments caused by a general loss of contact with reality. The company may become uncertain and confused about its direction, and part of the company may even fall apart prior to finding a new way of moving forward. On the other hand, positive Neptune transits can indicate a successful advertising campaign or the formulation of a new vision and direction for the company.

Pluto

Pluto is the major symbol of corporate power. It reveals the company's ability to transform itself by destroying the old and raising up the new. It also describes the hidden potential and assets of the business, and indicates whether power struggles are likely. Pluto also stands for the company's research and development ability. Pluto is associated with banking, finance, atomic energy and any underground or 'hidden' activities, such as tunnelling and mining.

By transit, Pluto can tear a company apart and bring about a process of transformation that will at times feel, and may even turn out to be, life-threatening. Difficult Pluto transits generally lead to major changes in company structure and the changes are so intense that sometimes even bankruptcy or liquidation result. Pluto transits can also suggest problems with debt, especially if Venus is also involved natally or by transit. A positive Pluto transit brings reorganisation, restructuring and the need to eliminate all that is no longer required; it can also signal the start of a major period of success. As Pluto moves so slowly, the changes it brings are always profound, with far-reaching, long-term effects. A major Pluto transit should *never* be ignored.

The Moon's Node
Natally, the Node indicates the alliances and associations of the business, showing how it relates to the general public and how it is perceived in return. Transits of the Node generally bring the company into the public eye or bring new business associations and links with other companies.

In addition to the planetary placements in the company chart, we also need to take into account the all-important angles: the Ascendant and the Midheaven.

The Ascendant
This stands for the company's environment, its shareholders and the manner in which it goes out to do business in the world.

The Midheaven
This is a vital point in the company chart, for it signifies the goals and directions of the business and what it is trying to achieve, as well as its public standing and the way it is seen by the public.

Major transits to the Midheaven invariably bring changes in the company's direction and can help (or hinder, depending on the nature of the transit) any re-orientation of the business that is already in progress at the time.

3. Aspects in the Company Chart

Each company birthchart has an individual set of aspects, determined by the planetary patterns at the time of incorporation. Readers will by now be familiar with the idea that hard aspects – notably squares and oppositions – are 'difficult', and flowing aspects – trines and sextiles – are 'good'. These traditional classifications hold good when considering the economy and the stock market, but when we come to assess how the aspects operate in company birthcharts, the situation is more complex and these broad principles need to be further refined.

Although the presence of squares and oppositions in a company birthchart may indeed indicate problems and obstacles, these can actually be quite positive, as they act as spurs to development, and are therefore the main way the business moves forward and grows. Squares in particular can indicate that the company is very dynamic, for these aspects tend to produce events to which the business must respond, and consequently generate the energy needed to propel the business forward. Trines can also indicate success, but the problem here is that life can often seem too easy for the business, and motivation can consequently be lacking. Although trines are traditionally benefic aspects, they generally lack the energy and drive of oppositions and squares. Business is not about 'the easy life' – or sitting back and being passive; in order to grow, a business needs to be dynamic and changing. Company charts with a concentration of trines produce businesses that take their good fortune for granted. This can remove the need to grow and develop, with the result that the business never realises its full potential. Some businesses with difficult aspects do of course fail, but those that can rise to the challenge frequently go on to become extremely successful companies, with well-known names.

COMPANY ASTROLOGY: FIVE CASE-STUDIES

The best way to understand how company astrology works is to see how the potentials of the birthchart unfold and work themselves out in the day-to-day process of business in the real world. The fortunes of every company fluctuate as it is periodically subject to expansive planetary transits from Jupiter or the testing transits of Saturn, Neptune and Pluto. As with the stock market, other astrological factors, such as eclipses and the faster-moving planets, also have a key role to play in company development, and must always be taken into account.

In the following pages we will look at five detailed case studies that illustrate the cyclical patterns of astrology at work within a selection of world-class corporations: Polly Peck, Next, Virgin Atlantic, Amstrad and Apple. These company profiles show how each company responded to the planetary challenges presented at key points in its history and either rose to the occasion – or did not. Our five corporate examples clearly show how the company chart acts as a kind of business 'road-map', with the transiting aspects showing the times when either difficult days or good opportunities lie ahead, and can thus be an invaluable aid to business planning.

1. Polly Peck

In the boom years of the 1980s, Polly Peck was constantly in the news, thanks to its high-flying share price; it was one of the stock market stars of the decade. In the 1990s too, the company has seldom been far from the headlines – but this time on account of its spectacular collapse. The tangled web surrounding the company's downfall has provided rich pickings for journalists world-wide and with every month that passes, there are new revelations in the nation's press. Looking at the company from the perspective of financial astrology reveals many insights into why the Polly Peck empire crashed in such a dramatic manner. But to unravel all the elements of the saga and to understand how the seeds of disaster were sown, we need to go back to the late 1950s, when the Polly Peck story began …

Like so many companies, Polly Peck is often identified with its chairman, Asil Nadir, but the business existed as a quoted company long before Nadir appeared on the scene. Polly Peck was incorporated on 22 June 1959 and the company chart is shown in Fig. 6.1. Before looking at the various planetary transits and other factors that resulted in such an abrupt reversal of Polly Peck's fortunes, we need to look at the natal chart in some detail, as this reveals the basic structure of the company and sets the scene for our analysis.

In the Polly Peck chart, three major aspect patterns immediately catch the eye. The first grouping is a close conjunction of Mars, Uranus and Venus in Leo. So what do the planets mean? What do they tell us about the company? What issues do they raise?

In the birthchart, natal Mars stands for the basic motivation, drive and energy of the company, Venus represents its resources, the assets of the company, particularly its financial assets, and Uranus symbolises its innovative ability and new ideas, as well as the desire to be different and stand out from the crowd. The grouping of the planets in this way suggests that the business will be very volatile, with sudden changes in the energy and drive of the company, and unexpected changes in the way it uses its financial assets. It also indicates a company with a fast-moving share price – albeit not always upwards. The configuration suggests that the company will be very fast-moving and develop rapidly when the time is right.

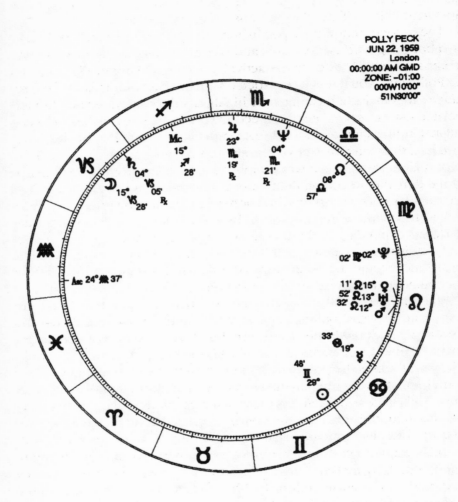

FIGURE 6.1: POLLY PECK

This important cluster of planets also trines the Midheaven (the goals and direction of the business) offering the company the potential to successfully use its powerful financial innovatory skills and drive to achieve its objectives – although since the trine can be a 'lazy' aspect, these innate abilities will need to be consciously harnessed.

The second important aspect is Jupiter square the Ascendant. Jupiter symbolises growth, expansion and the profit-making potential of the company, as well its overseas activities. (Readers will recall that much of Polly Peck's business was carried on outside the UK.) This square produces two major effects. First, it highlights the importance of Jupiter-related issues for the company. Secondly, it emphasises the link between all that Jupiter symbolises and the Ascendant – which stands for the shareholders, the company's environment and the way it is perceived in the world. Square aspects always imply that the company will experience some difficulty in getting the two principles involved to work together, but that efforts made in this direction will ultimately be productive. This suggests that the company would be seen as a growth stock, with the business expanding and growing over a period of time. A natal aspect only indicates a potential – in this case, the potential to be seen as a growth stock and the potential for the shares to rise. In order to realise its potential, the company must also work to bring it about.

The third noteworthy aspect is the trine between Saturn in Capricorn and Pluto in Virgo, potentially a very favourable grouping. In business astrology, Saturn indicates restriction, but it also stands for the management or board of directors, as well as basic company structure, whilst Pluto symbolises the power behind the business and its ability to transform itself at a very fundamental level. The natal Saturn–Pluto trine suggests Polly Peck had the ability to make major changes in its structure and organisation, thus giving it the ability to meet changing conditions and new opportunities by evolving and transforming its structures as required.

This company chart clearly shows great promise, with the latent potential of a high-flying share price all set to be realised once the company had made the requisite effort. In 1980, before Asil Nadir came on the scene, Polly Peck was a quoted company going nowhere, a penny stock with a share price of 9p. The buoyant share potential revealed in the natal chart was languishing unseen, awaiting the right astrological trigger. And on 16 February 1980, the necessary catalyst appeared, in the shape of a total solar eclipse.

In Chapter 5, we saw the powerful effects that eclipses can produce in the stock market when they contact transiting planetary configurations. In just the same way, there are certain companies – of which Polly

Peck is undoubtedly one – that respond very strongly to eclipses and the fortunes of the company can turn quite dramatically when an eclipse falls on a sensitive point in the company chart.

It is not overstating the case to say that eclipses provide the key to understanding the major developments, both positive and negative, in Polly Peck's chequered history. But the company did not crash simply because of an eclipse. Several other important planetary factors were also influencing the course of events and, as always in financial astrology, it is necessary to look at the whole picture. But first, let's examine that first positive eclipse in more detail.

The eclipse of February 1980 at 26 ≈ 50 ushered in a period of rapid expansion, as it fell within two-and-a-half degrees of the Ascendant and square to Jupiter, activating the growth potential of the natal Jupiter–Ascendant square. At the same time, Venus, the planet of money, was hitting the important point midway between the Sun and Moon – symbolically, the core of the business – and Mercury was squaring the Midheaven. Mercury transits often bring news about the company and on this occasion, the company announced its new future goals and direction. Nadir made an offer to inject one of his business interests (cardboard box manufacturing) into the company and in return acquired a large block of shares at 9p.

As the deal was finalised in March 1980, Uranus, the planet of sudden change, was close to a conjunction with natal Jupiter, the planet of success. This electrifying contact galvanised the company into almost-instantaneous growth. To complete the picture, transiting Jupiter came conjunct the company's natal Pluto the same month, thus providing an opportunity for Polly Peck to contact its hidden resources, assets and power. Although the February eclipse was not the sole cause of Polly Peck's sudden transformation, it locked in all the other influences, such as the Uranus transit to natal Jupiter and Jupiter transit to natal Pluto, and opened the door to the expansionist mode of operating that governed all company policy for several years to come.

That spring, a striking change in Polly Peck's market presence was visible to all. The shares, which could have been (and were) bought for 9p in March, rocketed to a year's high of 191p, and closed the year at 150p, having soared by 2,000 per cent at the peak in only nine months. A speculator's dream, or so it seemed. Throughout the early and mid-1980s, Polly Peck consolidated and maintained its reputation as a glamour stock, as it seemed to have mastered the enviable art of producing growth, rising profits and a perpetually rising share price. But as the Eighties drew to a close, formidable slow-moving planetary transits were lining up to challenge the business as never before.

On 7 September 1989, Polly Peck announced that it was to buy the fresh fruit division of Del Monte, a purchase that would be partly financed by a rights issue to raise £283 million. On the surface, this may have seemed like simply the latest in a long line of acquisitions, but the upcoming transits to the company chart revealed very clearly that dangerous days lay ahead. At this time, the two business planets, Jupiter (at 6 ♋ 52) and Saturn (at 7 ♑ 18), were in opposition, both closely squaring the company's Node – the indicator of alliances and associations with others. Note that this was indeed an alliance, for it was an agreed purchase rather than a takeover battle. The natal Node was further highlighted, as transiting Mercury and Neptune were exactly square each other at 9 ♎ 40 and 9 ♑ 40 respectively. The Mercury conjunct the Node indicated an announcement or news of a new relationship for Polly Peck, but the Neptune square the Node raised questions and spelled a possible warning. Neptune symbolises dreams and ideals, but also confusion and delusion, so the chart showed a clear danger of the company's dreams dissolving into disarray. Neptune transits often bring a loss of contact with reality to a company's affairs; in this case, it turned out to be one new business too many. For the dream of expansion had indeed lost contact with reality.

Yet another Node link occurred that day, as the transiting Node came conjunct Polly Peck's Ascendant. The way the company goes out to the world (the Ascendant) was through the Node – its alliances and associations. The message of the chart was thus aptly illustrated by the company's new links with Del Monte. Finally, in the uncanny way that astrologers themselves are hard put to explain, the company chart exactly timed the Del Monte purchase. The official documents announcing the acquisition were lodged with the stock exchange and the announcement released at 2.20 p.m. At that precise moment, the transiting Midheaven (which moves though the full 360 degrees of the zodiac each day) was exactly at 7 degrees Libra – less than 2 degrees from the natal Node!

But what of the rights issue to raise the money required for the purchase? Although transiting Venus, the planet of money, was trining the company's Ascendant when the announcement was made and it looked as though raising the finance would present no problems, deeper issues were already involved. For the 12 months prior to the rights issue, transiting Pluto had been squaring the Polly Peck's natal grouping of Mars, Uranus and Venus trine the Midheaven. This had the effect of bringing the whole issue of the company's financial resources, drive and potential into sharp focus, and the fact that these areas were being highlighted by the potentially destructive square of Pluto embodied a powerful warning.

Pluto is associated with debt and the fact that transiting Pluto was making a square to the natal Venus, the planet of money, indicated that serious debt problems could result. Nadir proposed that the Del Monte acquisition – which was to cost some £557 million – was to be financed not just by the £283 million rights issue, but also by loan facilities, a very unwise move as it turned out. For any business, the periods surrounding Pluto–Venus squares are times for reducing the debt burden, not increasing it as Nadir proposed. The Pluto–Venus square indicates that Nadir could hardly have chosen a worse time to take on extra debt.

As we have seen, Polly Peck is a company that reacts very strongly to eclipses and whilst the Del Monte negotiations were still going on, long before any public announcement, a lunar eclipse occurred on 17 August 1989 with the Moon at 24 ≈ 12, within half a degree of the natal Ascendant. Again, an eclipse catalysed the company into growth and was undoubtedly the reason Nadir found the deal irresistible, despite the fact that Polly Peck's finances simply did not add up. The eclipse linked in powerfully to the Jupiter–Ascendant square, suggesting that the company would shortly be going out into the world to make a purchase. Meanwhile, however, the dream was already beginning to fade, as Polly Peck's stock market rating started to slip, despite Nadir's continued displays of public confidence.

By the end of the 1980s there were growing doubts about the future growth potential of the business and the Del Monte acquisition was to be the last expansionary move the company ever made. Within 12 brief months, the confusion wrought by Neptune's square to the Node and Pluto's square to the natal Venus had taken their inevitable toll.

The crunch, when it came, was triggered by yet another eclipse – this time the lunar eclipse of 6 August 1990, which linked powerfully into the company chart and promptly began to wreak havoc. We have already seen in Chapter 5 how this same eclipse caused substantial falls in both London and New York: its effects on Polly Peck were even more severe. At the eclipse, two pairs of planetary oppositions had formed into the difficult astrological configuration known as a Grand Cross. All the planets were in fixed signs, with the Sun at 13 ♌ 52, the Moon at 13 ≈ 52, Mars at 16 ♉ 6 and Pluto at 15 ♏ 1, which linked straight into the important planetary grouping of Mars, Uranus and Venus trine the Midheaven in the Polly Peck company chart. In addition, Saturn, the planet of restriction, was almost exactly hitting the point midway between the Ascendant and the Midheaven (a symmetric pattern similar to those we have seen in major stock market moves). This latter factor alone would have been enough to cause considerable trouble for the company, but it happened at the same time as the destructive eclipse. Hitting the area of Polly Peck's chart concerned with innovation, drive and direction, the eclipse locked in this destructive pattern. The warning to take cover was there, plainly visible for all to see. The exact conjunction of the transiting Sun with Polly Peck's natal Uranus, both at 13 ♌ 52, and opposed by the Moon at the eclipse, sparked off an extraordinary six-week chain of events that eventually brought the company down.

At a board meeting of Polly Peck on Sunday 12 August 1990, Nadir announced his intention of taking the company private. Aptly enough, Mercury was exactly square the Midheaven, signifying that news of the company's direction would be made public. On the following day the shares rose sharply in response to the news. Less than a week later, on Friday 17, just as the Sun (the company's head) opposed its Ascendant (the shareholders), Nadir announced that he had changed his mind and the offer would not go ahead. As the news was released, the share price began to collapse. On that day alone, they plummeted by 25 per cent.

On Monday 20 August, just as Saturn, the planet of institutional author- ity, came to an exact opposition to the company's Mercury, the planet of news and communication, the stock exchange began an inquiry into the events of the previous week, in particular the initial announcements made by Nadir. On 24 August, the inquiry published the results of its findings. Not surprisingly, they were highly critical of the chairman and the way he had made that initial announcement.

During this period, Mercury had moved on from the square to the Midheaven, turned retrograde and was moving direct again from 25 August. On Thursday 6 September, this planet of news returned to the *exact* position it had when the initial buyout announcement was made; Nadir made the rather startling pronouncement that since shares were now very cheap, he would purchase four million of them in the mar- ket! Mercury, returning to its exact position at the announcement of the buyout, triggered the intention again and a large purchase of shares was made. Not quite the buyout that he had originally intended, but a last, desperate attempt to support the share price. It did not succeed. The share price continued to fall.

The end came on Thursday 20 September. On that day alone, Polly Peck's shares fell by 50 per cent and were eventually suspended by the stock exchange.

As a final footnote, during the entire six-week period from the time of the eclipse on 6 August to the suspension on 20 September, Pluto, the planet of destruction and resurrection, was moving through an exact square of Venus, the company's assets and resources. This time, transiting Pluto brought death to the company, rather than transformation. This time there was to be no resurrection: the destruction was too final and complete.

The share price finally collapsed as the news emerged that the Serious Fraud Office (SFO) had questioned Asil Nadir and this is why we must leave the story at this point. Charges were brought against Nadir, who subsequently skipped bail and fled to Cyprus. As the whole affair is presently before the courts, we cannot comment further, except to observe the effects of two final eclipses, which underline once again the sensitivity of this company to these particular influences. On 21 May 1993, a solar eclipse occurred at 0♊31, square the company's Pluto, whilst transiting Saturn at 0♓01 was opposing the company's Pluto. Two weeks later, a lunar eclipse on 4 June, with the Moon at 13♐55, was right on the company's Midheaven. A fresh string of allegations concerning Nadir's contributions to the Conservative Party was made, along with accusations that he had stolen money from Polly Peck. A full astrological analysis of the company must, however, await the court case – an event which will undoubtedly hold the media's attention in thrall once more.

2. Next

The Next group grew out of the clothing company Hepworth and Son, which was incorporated in 1891. On 3 January 1986, the company name was changed to Next. This was the name by which the group then became well known in the high street and also under which the shares were traded on the stock exchange. When one company evolves out of another in this way, we might sometimes continue to use the original company chart. However, in this case the change of company name marked such a radical transformation of the company's style and image that it became, to all intents and purposes, a new company. So in the analysis that follows, it is appropriate to use the chart for the change to the 'new' company, whose 1986 chart is shown in Fig. 6.2.

Next was born on the crest of the consumer boom that gathered momentum in the mid-Eighties and in the beginning, all went well. Like the Body Shop, Sock Shop and Laura Ashley, the transformed Hepworth and Son became one of the great retailing success stories of the day, and the business expanded quickly, often by takeover, but in late 1987, it began to stall. The reasons for this slowdown can clearly be seen in the company chart.

Unlike Polly Peck, whose problems stemmed from its particular sensitivity to eclipses and a crushing sequence of Pluto transits, the

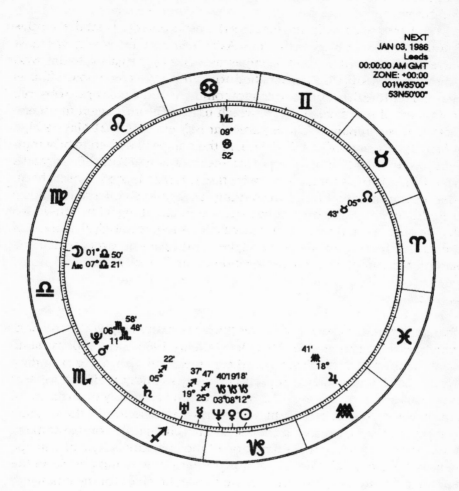

FIGURE 6.2: NEXT

astrological basis of the problems Next encountered during these years was primarily transiting Saturn. Transits of Saturn need not necessarily bring difficulties to a company, but they do indicate times when a business should slow down, take stock and consolidate its position. If a company is committed to growth, come what may, however – as Next was – the restrictions of Saturn will, almost inevitably, cause problems.

From the end of 1987 through most of 1988, thanks to the retrograde effect, Saturn made repeated conjunctions to Next's natal Mercury, the all-important planet of sales and trading. Had the company's management had the benefit of astrological insight, it would have known that this was a time to pull back, structure what it had and be content with maximising the retailing potential that already existed within the business. Instead, however, Next doggedly continued to expand – or at least, tried to. In January 1988, a mail order catalogue was launched. Since Mercury, which was currently being afflicted by Saturn, is also linked to postal services and mail order, the venture could not have been less timely. Far from generating the hoped-for profits, the mail order operation lost money from the outset. And just at this point, the economy began to slow down, thus eroding Next's general trading environment and profitability still further.

Things went from bad to worse: on 30 August 1988, when Saturn changed from retrograde to direct motion, the station at 25 ♐ 55 was less than one-sixth of a degree from Next's Mercury. The times when planets appear to stand still, or station, are particularly powerful moments. When stations aspect natal planets as closely as this, the effects are very powerful and far-reaching. The result here was that not only did sales suffer, but Next's share price also began to crumble and the company was one of the weakest performers on the UK Stock Exchange in 1988.

Still worse was to come in 1989, when Saturn moved on to conjunct natal Venus, symbol of the company's financial resources and money. From January to October 1989, Saturn made repeated conjunctions to the company Venus. Falling trade had by now led to growing debt and the company's cash flow – a very important manifestation of natal Venus – was under serious pressure. The downward movement in Next's share price continued and serious doubts about the long-term future of the business began to grow. In December 1990, to outside observers at least, the business seemed close to collapse. The shares had fallen to 6p and the company had a very serious debt problem to contend with. But behind the scenes, the beginnings of a recovery were at last coming together ...

Following the repeated transits of Saturn that had taken such a toll of the company over the past three years, 1990 brought some new and invigorating astrological influences to bear. Uranus, the planet of inspiration and sudden change, was repeatedly conjunct the company's Venus that year and also opposed the Midheaven, bringing new insights and innovation to the company's financial management and revitalising its general direction.

There were three oppositions between transiting Jupiter and Uranus around that time, which all proved to be powerfully beneficial as they contacted first Next's Moon – its relationship with the public – then Neptune and finally Venus and the Midheaven. The first opposition, in August 1989, had Jupiter at 1 ♋ 46 and Uranus at 1 ♑ 46, both within a fraction of a degree of squaring the Moon. This brought the innovation and expansion potential of these two transiting planets into contact with the Moon, the symbol of Next's customers and the products of the business. So although actual trading and financial conditions within the company were still in decline, the company was beginning to make moves to secure its future. Jupiter aspecting Uranus is a powerful combination and the fact that it contacted a natal point so exactly at the time of the opposition gave the company a real chance of coming through the crisis.

The second opposition, on 29 December 1989 at 5 ♋ 36/5 ♑ 36, made an important contact to natal Neptune at 3 ♑ 40 (the ideals and image of the company), and gave Next a new vision and the inspiration to move forward.

The final opposition, however, at 9 ♋ 14/9 ♑ 14 on 13 May 1990 was the key to restoring the company's finances to order as it fell within a degree of Next's natal Venus – its money, assets and financial resources. The opposition also fell close to Next's Midheaven, helping to give the company a totally new direction. To the outside world and watching investors, trading still looked poor and the company's public image had still not begun to recover. Yet behind the scenes, the company was making huge efforts to change and restructure.

The final piece of the jigsaw was provided by Pluto, the planet of transformation, which in late 1990 began to make three slow-moving squares to the company's natal Jupiter at 18 ♒ 41, which were to last until November 1991. Natal Jupiter shows the company's potential for growth and moneymaking – now subject to the transforming effect of Pluto. Since management had done the necessary groundwork, the powerful combination of Jupiter and Pluto did indeed transform Next's ability to grow. Readers should note the way different transits build up over a period, each one contributing either to the company's problems or to their solution. For it is important to consider this dynamically developing set of influences on the company, not just the influence of a single factor.

By 1991, the whole world could see that things were beginning to improve. Negotiations were begun to sell off one of the group's businesses, the Grattan mail order catalogue. Two bidders emerged and the price steadily rose. The deal was eventually concluded for £165 million. From an all-time low of 6p in December 1990, shares hit 45p in September 1991 and over 100p in September 1992, representing an improvement of over 800 per cent in just nine months. This showed how wrong-footed investors had been in their judgement that the business would not survive.

The stock market can hardly be blamed for its short-sighted attitude towards Next, however, for few speculators or City analysts had the benefit of knowing what favourable astrological influences were at work behind the scenes, helping the business to make a comeback. And it is not only investors who could have benefited from knowing about these planetary influences. With the insights of astrology, the company itself could have seen the difficult Saturn transits that were due to occur in late 1987 and 1988, and minimised the downturn in its fortunes by working with these restrictive influences rather than simply trying to ignore them.

3. Virgin Atlantic

We will now turn our attention to a privately-owned company, Virgin Atlantic, a trail-blazing airline headed by one of the most interesting entrepreneurs in the international business community – Richard Branson. Virgin Atlantic is part of the Virgin Group which Branson founded, an innovative set of companies with wide interests in the leisure and entertainment fields. Although other parts of the Group were, for a short time, publicly quoted, Virgin Atlantic has always been privately owned. It thus provides an interesting contrast with the public companies we have considered so far.

Virgin Atlantic was incorporated on 26 November 1981, and the company chart (shown in Fig. 6.3) provides an extremely good basis for a business with the avowed corporate goal of challenging the big national carriers. In the chart, Mercury, the planet of communication and travel, is conjunct the Moon, which stands for the public or Virgin's customers, indicating that the company will find favour as a mass carrier with the general public as a whole. Mercury and the Moon are also trine the Node, so the relationships of the business and how it is perceived are seen as being connected with transporting the public. Success for the business is also implicit in the fact that Pluto is square the Node, which

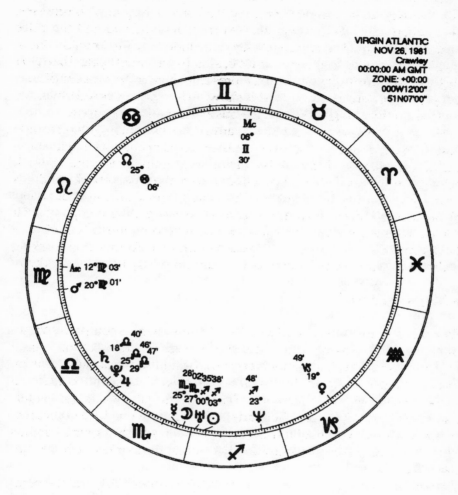

FIGURE 6.3: VIRGIN ATLANTIC

suggests that Virgin Atlantic has the potential to radically transform the way airlines operate and how they are viewed by the public at large.

Also significant is the position of Virgin Atlantic's Midheaven at 6 ♊ 30, which directly opposes an area of the zodiac long associated with aviation and flying. This astrological tradition dates back to 1903, when the chart set up for the first powered flight by the Wright brothers has the Midheaven at 5 ♐. On 1 January 1911, when the first commercial flight took off from St Petersburg, Florida, the Midheaven was once again around 5 ♐ and so this area of the zodiac was christened 'the degrees of flight'. The fact that Virgin Atlantic's Midheaven/IC axis is on these degrees provides a strong indication that it will be a key player in the airline business.

Further astrological pointers to success were present on the day of Virgin Atlantic's maiden flight from London to New York on 22 June 1984, which locked in the transiting planetary configurations of the day. Transiting Mercury at the end of Gemini was trining natal Jupiter, suggesting that transport would expand the business. In addition, transiting Pluto at 29 ♎ 23 was within half a degree of a conjunction with natal Jupiter, a powerful combination of planetary influences which played a key role in the recovery of Next. Here, too, the Jupiter–Pluto contact augured well: Virgin Atlantic was an overnight success. Since to all intents and purposes, the business really began on the day the maiden flight took place, the favourable transits on that day were locked in rather like a new natal chart and still influence the business to this day.

The business got off to a good start and during the summer of 1985 Virgin Atlantic's flights were 99.9 per cent full, despite a transit of Saturn over the natal Mercury. It might be thought that such a transit would have depressed trading but it had little impact on Virgin Atlantic – unlike Next – for two reasons. First, the Jupiter–Pluto contact was so powerful that it was not easily counteracted, at least in the short term. Second, although Saturn transited Mercury, it did not station close to it, unlike Next, where it stationed exactly conjunct Mercury and was thus so much more powerful than a simple contact. Since Virgin Atlantic was also consolidating its existing business during the summer of 1985, rather than attempting to expand and branch out – as Next had done – the company was, astrologically speaking, doing all the right things. It was working with the influences rather than against them and so no ill effects resulted.

In 1986, fears of terrorist activity in Europe led to a downturn in trans-Atlantic traffic, which affected all airlines flying the Atlantic. Virgin Atlantic responded by reducing fares; its cheapest single fare to New York was cut to just £56 in response to its main US rival, People Express, which had introduced a £66 fare. A price war then began between the two airlines. When this new cheap fare was announced on 3 June 1986, the transiting Node at 29 ♎ 22 was not only conjunct natal Jupiter, but was also just one-sixtieth of a degree from the position of Pluto at Virgin's first trans-Atlantic flight! In addition, the expansionary principle of transiting Jupiter in Pisces was opposing the energetic and fighting Mars, a clear indication of a battle ahead; that Jupiter moreover was sextile natal Venus also clearly indicated that it was a battle about money.

Virgin Atlantic's business continued to expand and grow, but rather than chart each event in its business history, we will consider a remarkable battle that developed in 1991. On 12 December 1991, Richard Branson made the astonishing announcement that a 'dirty tricks campaign' was being waged against Virgin Atlantic by British Airways; Branson also announced that he was sending letters of complaint to the UK and European airline regulatory authorities. He alleged that BA had set up a task force to discredit Virgin and had systematically approached Virgin's passengers to try to persuade them to fly with BA. Clearly some major transits had been affecting Virgin's chart over the past 12 months and a closer analysis reveals exactly what was happening. But the transits made at the time of the announcement were also noteworthy and we should take a brief look at those first.

At the time of the announcement, transiting Mercury was squaring the company's Ascendant, bringing news about the business – but since Mercury was also almost conjunct natal Neptune at 23 ♐ 48, the news concerned rumours, scandal and attempts to deceive and undermine the entire organisation.

As we have noted, the transits of Neptune to key points in a company's chart can cause problems due to scandal-mongering, rumours and deceit. Throughout 1991, transiting Neptune had repeatedly been making a semisquare (45 aspect) to the midway point between the Sun–Moon in Virgin's chart. This is a very sensitive point in any company's chart, as it represents the very heart of the business, that point where the company comes into contact with its customers. Although the semisquare (45 degrees) is not a major aspect, it is a 'hard' aspect none the less, and on this occasion, the Neptune semisquare proved capable of causing some considerable damage. We should also note that natal Uranus is also positioned on this focal midway point between the Sun and Moon, making it particularly sensitive to transits; sudden and unexpected events will occur under transits to this point. The whole world watched in incredulity as 'the world's favourite airline' and Virgin Atlantic engaged in a courtroom battle – from which Richard Branson emerged the clear victor.

Virgin Atlantic promises to be a very interesting company to watch during 1993 and 1994, as transiting Pluto, the planet of radical change and transformation, will be conjunct the airline's Moon (its customers) and Mercury (its selling and trading activities). Although Pluto conjunctions are not necessarily as stressful as squares, they inevitably bring deep, thoroughgoing changes to any business, and we can expect to see Virgin Atlantic depart significantly from its established ways of carrying out its travel business and also from the way it deals with the public. August 1994 will be a particularly important period, as Pluto stations at 25 ♏ 16 on 5 August, within a fraction of a degree from natal Mercury and trine the natal Node. As transiting Saturn is also opposing the Ascendant (the shareholders) we should certainly hear some important news about the business at that time.

4. Amstrad

The UK consumer electronics group Amstrad was founded by Alan Sugar, who was once dubbed 'Britain's greatest entrepreneur' and is one of the most innovative and dynamic figures on the British business scene. Amstrad's name is derived from Alan Sugar's initials – Alan Michael Sugar (Trading) – and the company was incorporated on 19 November 1968.

Amstrad's chart, which is illustrated in Fig. 6.4, shows a number of interesting astrological patterns. First, let's look at the group of planets in Libra – Jupiter, Uranus and Mars. This important conjunction combines the expansiveness and energy of Jupiter and Mars with the innovative and inventive brilliance of Uranus. Uranus is also strongly associated with electronics and so its conjunction with Jupiter is a promising placement for a business like Amstrad. This planetary grouping is opposed by the Node, which stands for the business's associations and how it is viewed in general. This suggests that Amstrad will have a good, innovative image – a great asset for a company operating in the field of electronics. This triad of planets also forms a square aspect to Venus in Capricorn, the planet of money and finance. The overall pattern, although not necessarily easy, is certainly a very dynamic one and clearly indicates excellent potential for financial growth and innovative development. As suggested by its chart, Amstrad did in fact grow extremely fast, and during the 1970s and 1980s it became one of Europe's market leaders in the production of audio equipment and, latterly, computers. The Amstrad PCW was truly innovative, for it introduced many people to computers for the first time and served to make word processing accessible to the general public.

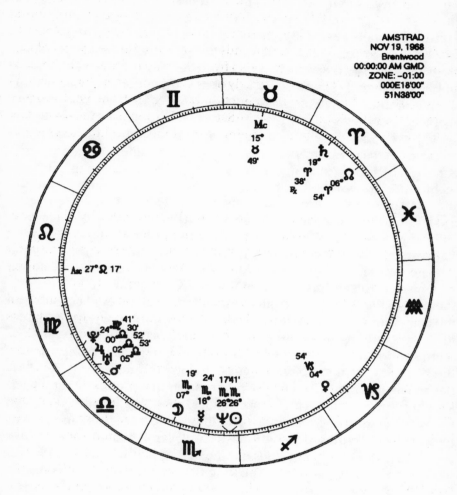

FIGURE 6.4: AMSTRAD

There is, however, one feature in the chart that gives immediate cause for concern. Saturn, the planet of structure and stability, does not link in to any other planets in the chart, which would lead us to suspect there might be problems in producing the kind of structures and controls that the business required. Such a lack of structure was exemplified by the fact that for many years the company's top management all worked from one large open-plan office, with Sugar himself barking orders to his staff from a battered leather armchair in the centre of the room! In 1992, Sugar publicly admitted that Amstrad lacked the structures and systems normally found in a large international company of the size Amstrad had, by then, become.

Here we can see the importance of analysing both the strengths and weaknesses that are latent in the company chart. A planet such as Amstrad's Saturn, which makes no major aspects to anything else in the chart, is technically known as an 'unaspected planet' and its appearance in the chart denotes an area of the business that should be given special attention. Although an unaspected Saturn in the natal chart is not in itself sufficient to cause problems, it does suggest that creating the right company structure will never be easy for Amstrad, and that the business will have to consciously work to develop and regularly update its internal systems, controls and management abilities. Amstrad's chart clearly shows the danger that growth through constant innovation would consume all the company's time and energy, and that building appropriate management structures might consequently be overlooked.

It is important to reiterate at this point that particular placements in the company chart in no way suggest that the business is 'fated'. Many businessmen in the UK have discovered, on the contrary, that understanding and working with the astrological chart can help their business to make the most of its strengths and they can take steps to mitigate its weaknesses. The presence of an unaspected planet, as in Amstrad's chart, indicates a weak spot, but does not mean that problems are inevitable. Rather, it is a warning signal, showing that this area of the business is unlikely to integrate easily with the company's other activities, and care should be taken not to ignore it. If the warning is heeded and appropriate steps taken, no problems need arise. Working with the company chart in this way helps avoid any hazards or pitfalls that may be present in the company's astrological profile.

Having begun its trading career by selling audio and consumer electronic equipment, Amstrad moved into the home computer market in April 1984. Right from the outset, Amstrad's computers looked like professional business machines and the growth potential of this new direction was aptly reflected by the transits of the time. From January to October 1984, transiting Jupiter was in early Capricorn, making repeated conjunctions with natal Venus and squaring the Node and the dynamic Jupiter–Uranus–Mars grouping. This transit unlocked the huge potential for growth by innovation symbolised by this natal grouping and set Amstrad firmly on the road to expansion. The profits from computer sales rapidly dwarfed those from the audio business and Amstrad's share of the personal computer market in the UK soon equalled that of its arch rival, IBM.

Amstrad's impressive growth was naturally reflected in its share price, which began a very strong rise in 1985. At the end of April 1985, the shares were 77p and later that year they reached a high of 202p. By February 1986, they had climbed to over 350p; in May they were 550p and later reached the year's high point, equivalent to 770p. The astrological causes for this meteoric rise in share price can be ascribed to the favourable influence of Jupiter, which coincided with the triggering effects of not just one, but two eclipses. As we saw in the preceding chapter, eclipses can produce very sharp moves in share prices and this is precisely what happened in this case. On 4 May 1985, a lunar eclipse occurred with the Sun at 14 ♉ 17 and the Moon at 14 ♏ 17, lying right across the Midheaven/IC axis and also close to natal Mercury, the planet of trading, at 16 ♏ 24. Also at this time, Jupiter at 15 ♒ 27 was squaring both Mercury and the Midheaven. On 19 May, a second eclipse occurred at 28 ♉ 50, within two degrees of an exact square to the Ascendant (the shareholders). By the time of this second eclipse, Jupiter had moved on to 16 ♒ 33 and was almost exactly square to natal Mercury. A further factor that reinforced these powerful eclipses was the fact that up until September 1986, transiting Pluto was sextile natal Venus, indicating that the company's finances were being transformed in a highly positive way. We will see these two eclipses again in our next example, Apple Inc., but there different natal planets were involved and so the results were very different.

The next step for Amstrad was overseas expansion, and in 1987 the company set up subsidiaries in France, Germany, Spain and Hong Kong. But since the company's structures and financial controls – reflected by its weak natal Saturn – could not keep pace with this kind of expansion, trouble lay ahead. In May 1987, transiting Jupiter opposed Amstrad's Saturn and in December it stationed within 10 minutes of arc from the exact opposition. Also in 1987, transiting Uranus, the planet of sudden changes, and in this case 'sudden expansion', was making three squares to Amstrad's natal Pluto, symbol of the company's power and its ability to transform itself. Finally, as is so frequently the case at crucial times in a company's history, transiting Pluto was bringing radical changes too. In July 1987, it stationed at 7 ♏︎ 9, almost exactly conjunct Amstrad's natal Moon, which signified its employees. The company that had formerly run its operation with a skeletal staff now found itself with an international workforce of 1,600. Overseas expansion had also brought soaring costs and it soon became clear that growth had been too rapid; as the new year dawned in 1988 Amstrad's financial problems were beginning to mount.

Alan Sugar was later to call 1988 Amstrad's 'Year of Disaster', for this was the watershed year when the company's profits actually fell for the first time in its history. Astrologically, the roots of the problem can be traced to February 1988, when transiting Saturn and Uranus – a combination that often brings sudden restriction – were conjunct at 29 ♐︎ 56, less than a degree from Amstrad's natal Jupiter, the company's profit-making potential. By April, Saturn had moved on to station in an almost exact square to the natal Uranus, which restricted Amstrad's innovative ability. This naturally spelled severe problems for a company engaged in developing such typically Uranus-ruled products as computers and electronics. The restrictive effects of Saturn continued to be felt until it made its final square to natal Jupiter and natal Uranus at the end of 1988.

But 1989 brought yet another round of problems to the beleaguered business, as Amstrad's Venus, symbol of its financial and monetary resources, was in turn hit by conjunctions from transiting Saturn and Uranus, resulting in sudden financial losses. Sugar's importunate overseas expansion meant that the company, which had previously operated from a cash-positive base, now suddenly had debts totalling some £100 million.

Still more problems lay in store for Amstrad in 1989, as transiting Neptune began to oppose the point midway between Jupiter and Saturn. Natal Jupiter and Saturn are both fundamental to a company's activities, and so the point that lies midway between them is highly sensitive to influences that may affect its long-term development and success. Neptune can be a very difficult influence for a company to deal with, as it tends to undermine and confuse whatever it contacts, and Neptune's repeated transit over the Jupiter–Saturn midpoint in Amstrad's chart led, as would be expected, to confusion and mistakes. On 20 April, with transiting Mercury exactly on the Midheaven and opposing natal Mercury, Amstrad announced problems with its new PC2000 range of computers; in July, 7,000 of these computers were recalled due to a chip problem.

We do not have sufficient space here for a full discussion of Amstrad's return from the brink, but as transiting Pluto neared the natal IC (thus opposing the Midheaven) and the natal Mercury, Amstrad's planet of trading, the company began to renew itself from its very foundations. Alan Sugar began radically to transform and strengthen Amstrad's internal structures, as these were now widely recognised as being urgently in need of improvement. The group's unprofitable foreign subsidiaries in Spain and America were closed down, and stocks were drastically reduced. At the same time, senior management was greatly strengthened, and a new system of inventory and financial controls introduced. Amstrad resisted media attempts to consign it to the scrap-heap and by 1990 the company was once again making a modest profit.

Looking ahead to the future, it is likely that 1994 will see major changes in store for Amstrad. Beginning in December 1993 and continuing throughout the whole of 1994, Pluto will repeatedly be conjunct Amstrad's natal Sun and square its Ascendant, thus indicating major changes in both the external perception of the company and also in the way it is led. The ground has been laid for these changes by the repeated squares to Amstrad's natal Saturn made by Uranus and Neptune throughout 1993; the last of these squares took place in November/December and they are bound to produce results in 1994. Combined with the effect of the Pluto transit, we would definitely expect to see changes in Amstrad's structures and also in its leadership. *Not* necessarily a change of leader, but certainly a change in the *way* the business is led and controlled, which will bring about a corresponding change in the way Amstrad is externally perceived.

5. Apple Computer Inc.

Each of the companies we have looked at so far has had its own highly individual style of business and Apple Computer Inc. is no exception. Indeed, Apple has long been renowned in the global business community for its unique and ground-breaking approach to corporate life.

Apple's founders and employees set out with a mission. This mission – one they continue to pursue – was to change the world by bringing 'computer power' to the people. The whole structure and organisation of Apple is more like a university department than a Fortune 500 company, and is characterised by informality, the desire to innovate and a predominantly youthful workforce. These qualities have served to create a new kind of business ethos, which is reflected in the network of satellite or 'spin-out' companies that surround the founder company, Apple.

Apple's innovative approach is a prominent feature of its incorporation chart (Fig. 6.5), which is worth looking at in some detail. There are several major aspect patterns. The first is a trine between Saturn (structure) and Neptune (ideals), which shows both the easy structuring of ideals and the ability to manifest them, but also the somewhat diffuse and nebulous company structure. This aspect is double-edged: in the case of an idealistic company such as Apple it can be a great strength, but it is also a potential source of problems, as we will see later.

The next aspect to consider is the Sun closely square Pluto, which suggests that the company has a great deal of power, intensity and the ability to transform, which stems from the leaders and founders of the company. Although this may sound like a good aspect to have, it is nevertheless a very difficult one to handle, as it suggests that power struggles may take place within the company, and it is not surprising that the original founders (the Sun) are today no longer associated with the business. That was the price Apple had to pay for its ability to transform.

The third aspect of note is an almost exact trine between Venus and the Node, which expresses itself in two ways. Venus is the planet of money and resources, and allied here in easy aspect to the Node (associations and relationships), it aptly describes the network of spin-out businesses surrounding Apple. This network has created a synergy whereby both sides make money. The Venus–Node trine also describes the fact that very many Apple employees have become millionaires through their association with the company, by virtue of their stock options.

The most dangerous and forbidding aspect in the natal chart, however, is the 135-degree aspect between Pluto and Venus, which is almost exact, being within three minutes of arc. We have seen this difficult planetary combination at work in earlier case studies and its presence in the natal chart locks in the destructive potential of Pluto to the company's finances. On the positive side, it also locks in enormous power and this is one reason why Apple has become so wealthy. The Pluto–Venus aspect will either bring the company great wealth, as in Apple's case, or will totally destroy it.

Three other patterns in the company's natal chart also hold the key to Apple's unusual nature and these involve the points midway between two natal planets, which are otherwise known as 'midpoints'.

First, the Sun–Moon midpoint, which describes the very heart of the business, is at 0 degrees Aries, an extremely powerful position. This is the starting point of the zodiac, a point associated with the people of the world as a whole, thus describing Apple's core mission to 'change the world'.

Second, Mars, the planet of energy and drive, falls halfway between Mercury and Neptune, showing that imagination and vision form an essential part of the identity and individuality of the company as a whole.

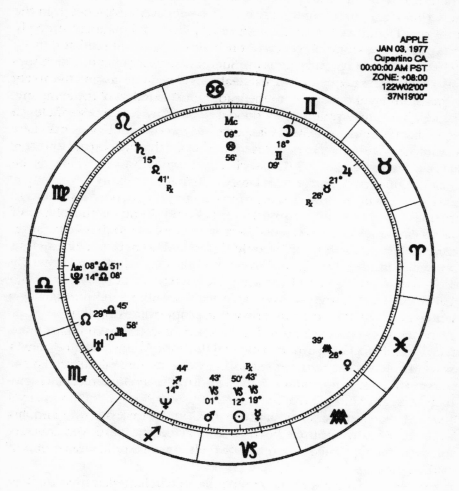

FIGURE 6.5: APPLE

Third, a further factor involving idealism is brought into play by the positioning of natal Pluto, the planet of transformation and power, on the midway point between Saturn and Neptune – a point that can be described as 'structuring the dream'. This suggests the power available to Apple from making its dreams a reality via its products.

Apple's incorporation charts speaks strongly of a mission and this is what seems to have provided inspiration not only for its founders, but also for their many employees. Its chart is not an easy one, but the process of living out and embodying its unusual features in the market-place has made Apple the world-class company it is today. Taking a more conventional, 'big business' approach would not have worked for a company with this chart. Apple lives out its chart to the full and so it has succeeded.

Space does not permit a full history of Apple's company development and so we will confine ourself to looking at the effects of one major business cycle on the organisation: the 30-year cycle of Saturn. In pre-vious examples, we have seen the powerful effects that Saturn transits can produce when they aspect important planets or natal positions. Here, we will consider the influence of the cycle as a whole and how it is reflected in external events.

The cycle of Saturn in relation to its natal position is extremely impor-tant for a business. When Saturn is square, opposition or (after 30 years) conjunct its natal position, there will often be a crisis within the busi-ness, usually focusing on structure and future development. As we have seen, Apple's natal Saturn is also trine Neptune and so the transits of Saturn will also tend to raise issues or questions concerning the com-pany's dreams and ideals.

Apple was founded on 3 January 1977 and transiting Saturn square its natal position occurred in 1984. This marked a major time of crisis for the company. The second half of 1983 saw a general fall in demand for PCs, Apple's included. Earlier, in February 1983, Pluto had stationed in trine to natal Venus, symbol of Apple's financial resources. Stations, as we have seen, are very powerful events, but the trine aspect is not usually financially fatal. It did, however, mark the start of a serious finan-cial downturn for the business, reflected in falling demand and reduced sales. In October 1983, Pluto trined Venus again, just as *Business Week* declared that IBM had won the PC race and Apple was out of contention.

In November 1983, Apple's fortunes appeared to revive, but this was to be only a temporary respite. With Jupiter conjunct natal Neptune, sug-gesting successful advertising, and then opposition the Moon (symbolising the public), Apple put together a major television advert. The advert was screened during the Superbowl in January 1984, when a classic 'advertising configuration' was in operation. Transiting Jupiter conjunct transiting Neptune had moved on to the midway point between natal Venus (money) and the node (associations), making a sextile aspect to both these planets. The advert was a huge success, winning several awards for its innovative approach and ground-breaking style.

The Apple II computer had always been the mainstay of the company's sales, but following a lull in the Pluto–Venus transits, the new Macintosh computer made its appearance in January 1984. With the company's brave new advertising campaign to support the launch, all seemed to go well. Jupiter (expansion and success) was conjunct natal Mars (drive and energy). But throughout 1984 the seven-year Saturn square was making itself felt. In addition, in November 1983, and again in June and August 1984, transiting Saturn had made repeated conjunctions to Apple's Uranus, its symbol of innovation and originality. Since Uranus is also associated with computers and Saturn almost invariably brings some form of restriction, it's no surprise to learn that around the same time Apple began to experience serious delays with many of the planned enhancements to its new Mac range.

The crisis at Apple gathered momentum in late 1984, as the company's structure and ideals (the Saturn/Neptune issue) came under scrutiny. In February, May and December 1984, transiting Neptune was in 135-degree aspect to natal Saturn, and the fluid company structure suggested by its natal Saturn–Neptune trine was now subject to further undermining by transiting Neptune. Unfortunately, this coincided with the gathering pressure on management and structures from the seven-year Saturn square, and the cumulative effect was disastrous. In late 1984 the whole management structure started to fall apart.

In December 1984, Saturn opposed natal Jupiter, restricting further Apple's ability to make profits. Sales remained weak, and by early 1985, many senior executives and key employees were resigning. The company was in crisis.

From an astrological point of view, the low point of this crisis occurred on 25 July 1985, when Saturn stationed in opposition to natal Jupiter. But happily, by this point Apple had begun to take on board the lessons of the Saturn transits. On 14 June 1985, drastic, but appropriate, measures were taken to avert disaster. The workforce was cut by 20 per cent and three factories were closed. In addition, Apple announced its first-ever quarterly loss as a public company. The shock to Apple's employees was profound, but the planetary background to this difficult time was evident to those who were cognisant with Apple's astrological background.

Two months prior to the announcement, on 4 May 1985, a lunar eclipse occurred, which linked in to the company's chart in a rather difficult way. The Moon at 14 ♏ 17 and Sun at 14 ♉ 17 (in the middle of the fixed signs) were squaring Apple's natal Saturn, clearly indicating the need for restriction, a need it would have been dangerous to ignore. Two weeks later, a second (solar) eclipse at 28 ♉ 50 formed an almost exact square (within a quarter of a degree) to Apple's Venus (money and resources). Several weeks later, the cutbacks were announced. It is interesting to note that during both eclipses, transiting Jupiter was opposing natal Saturn, indicating that the crisis point had been reached and that thereafter matters might improve.

At the time of the 14 June announcement, transiting Mercury and Mars were both opposing natal Mars, bringing news about Apple's ability to take decisive action. As transiting Neptune was also conjunct natal Mars, shock and confusion were the main reactions of the workforce.

The drastic measures of June 1985 achieved the desired effect and, having responded in an appropriate way to the challenge of the Saturn square, Apple's business recovered quickly. From a market capitalisation of $900 million in June 1985, it reached $5.5 billion by spring 1987.

The next major challenge to the company came, suitably enough, when transiting Saturn opposed Apple's natal Saturn in the summer of 1992. During this year, Apple was forced to undertake a complete restructuring and re-engineering of its products in response to the challenge presented by the cheaper computers of its rivals, such as Novell and Sharp. Customers were no longer prepared to pay a high price for an Apple computer when they could obtain an equivalent machine elsewhere at much lower cost.

As for the future, 1994 sees transiting Jupiter make three conjunctions to Apple's Uranus; in addition a solar eclipse on 3 November 1994 at 10 ♏ 54 falls within a fraction within a degree of natal Uranus. A major innovation is to be expected from Apple during late 1994 or early 1995.

SUMMARY

We have seen various planetary transits at work in company charts and it may be helpful to summarise some points to be kept in mind when looking at the prospects for a company.

1. Saturn brings restriction: when contacting natal Mercury sales slow down; when natal Venus is involved, cash flow and financial resources will be under pressure. Retrench and consolidate at these times, do not expand.

2. Pluto brings major changes. Never ignore a Pluto transit, rather look to reorganise radically or even see an ending in the area it contacts.

3. Pluto contacts to natal Venus warn of debt problems: reduce debt before they happen.

4. Jupiter brings expansion and growth: make use of its transits. For example, Jupiter conjunct natal Mercury is a good time to expand the business.

5. Watch where outer planets make stations. If they aspect a natal planet closely then that area of the business will be strongly highlighted.

6. Eclipses making close aspects to natal planets also strongly emphasise the issues associated with those planets. Look out for them well in advance and take appropriate measures.

What the Future Holds: Financial Predictions to the Year 2000 and Beyond

In this book we have shown how the tools and techniques of financial astrology can be used to identify and predict both the long-term and short-term cycles at work in the economy, the stock market and individual businesses. Whilst using astrology to predict the future can be of inestimable benefit in every area of business and finance, it must be emphasised once again that financial astrology is not concerned with preordained events, but with likelihood and probability. Astrology is a tool, not a crutch, and should always be used in that spirit.

Financial astrology is in essence a form of deductive reasoning, for it uses the past as a guide to the future. By looking at the financial and economic events that have repeatedly corresponded with particular planetary patterns and cycles in the past, we can formulate indications of what is likely to occur in the years to come. This is the basis for our forecasts which are set out below.

These predictions represent the balance of probabilities, and should be read and referred back to bearing this in mind. Financial astrology is by no means an exact science, but it does provide an excellent way of discerning the likely pattern of events. It can also, at times, be remarkably accurate ...

THE ECONOMY

Looking at the long-term cycles picture, we can see that the recession of the early 1990s has at last come to an end in the UK and the US. Recovery, however, is likely to be both slow and weak. In the UK, recovery will be promoted and encouraged by helpful astrological influences in April and August 1994, and this will provide the cue for *sustained* growth, which we predict will begin in mid-1994. By 1995, both the UK and US economies should be firmly back on the path of growth. Although the general level of economic activity will be subject to its usual ups and downs, we do not foresee another major recession this decade. In the US, we note that the McWhirter Node cycle is now well past its low point, giving a further indication of recovery.

In 2001, however, the cycles picture indicates the strong likelihood of yet another serious recession. This is because, in the UK, the Jupiter–Uranus cycle will be in its falling phase and the Jupiter–Pluto cycle will have hit a peak, prior to turning down. Both these cycles are crucial to the UK and US economy, and as their falling phases coincide and reinforce each other, a new recession will begin.

In the US, however, we predict that recession will not begin until 2002, as the Jupiter–Pluto cycle has a different shape and timing in America, and hits a peak later than in the UK. The likelihood is therefore that Britain will go into recession first, followed some 12–18 months later by the US. The first recession of the new millennium is likely to be severe and protracted, and it is unlikely that growth will be restored until 2004–5.

Returning to the present day, the growth that will take place over the next six or seven years should rebuild many of the businesses that were hit so badly by the last recession, but entrepreneurs and investors alike should watch out for the warning signs as the year 2000 approaches. Any sign of major speculative excess or the general attitude that 'the new millennium is bound to bring sustained economic prosperity' or 'growth will continue indefinitely' or, again, 'growth is here for good' is the clearest possible indication that trouble lies ahead. As in the 1980s, an economic climate of boundless optimism and a widely held view in business circles that 'things cannot go wrong' is in fact the most reliable indicator that a new recession lies just around the corner.

As we stated in Chapter 3, our longest-range forecast for the global economy is that a severe recession – akin to that of the 1990s – will take place in 2050. We predict that this will be one of the severe 'every 60 years' recessions, since 2050 is the next occasion on which the Jupiter–Saturn triple cycle hits the crucial point that always triggers a major downturn. As this lies so far in the future, however, we are sure it will give our readers little cause for concern!

INFLATION

As noted in Chapter 3, we predict that UK inflation will be at a low point in mid-1993. From this point onwards we expect it to rise gradually, particularly once recovery is well under way in 1994–5. There are no indications that inflation will move to unduly high levels, but a rate of around six per cent looks possible by 1996, and we expect inflation to peak at around seven–eight per cent in 1997.

Our forecast is based on the fact that all the UK inflation cycles reached their low point at around the same time in 1993, causing inflation to hit bottom. The long-term cycles take 10–15 years to reach their high point, but the shorter-term ones will be rising over the next few years.

THE PROPERTY MARKET

The one really bright note in the economy relates to house prices. Happily, the housing slump of the last few years now appears to be well and truly over!

Back in the halcyon days of 1988 when it seemed to all intents and purposes that property prices would carry on rising indefinitely, the lone voice of a UK astrologer was heard to say that the bubble was about to burst. Earlier that year, astrologer Charles Harvey had noted that the impending Saturn–Neptune conjunction which took place at the same time as the Jupiter–Saturn triple cycle opposition would not just cause a major recession but also depress house prices in the UK for some considerable length of time. Although few people were prepared to listen to him at the time, the events of recent years have shown how precise his description of future conditions turned out to be.

Harvey's prediction for UK house prices was based on the fact that Saturn – which generally brings restriction and falling prices – happened, at the time of the Jupiter–Saturn opposition and Neptune conjunction, to fall in that part of the UK national chart which is associated with homes and housing. Fortunately, Saturn has now moved out of this area and, coupled with the rise in economic activity which will take place in 1994, we predict that property prices should start rising again around this time.

THE UK STOCK MARKET

Our chronological round-up of predictions for the UK stock market begins in September 1994. We expect the UK market to make a low in August 1994 and a rise to begin on 1 September. The solar cycle indicator usually works to counter any strong rise at this time of year and September is normally a weak month for the market. In 1994, however, a transiting Jupiter–Saturn trine will be triggered by the Sun and past experience shows that strong rises are generally produced whenever this occurs.

A further rise can be expected thanks to the action of the four-year solar cycle in early 1995. Using this cycle as a guide, 1995 is a 'strong rise' year. Remember that the market has risen in every one of these years since 1947. This type of bull market usually begins in late December and lasts until April or sometimes June, so the period from December 1994 to April 1995 should certainly see the market rise. The size of the rise varies to a certain extent – some years the rise is small, some years large – but so far a market rise has always occurred.

Moving on to 1996, we expect the 'New Year Rally' to be quite weak that year, due to the effect of the Mercury–Uranus cycle, which peaks in early 1996. The cycles picture also leads us to expect that the market will be quite weak until August 1996.

Earlier we saw how the market can move quite dramatically when the transiting angles hit certain planetary patterns and a notable instance of this will take place in 1996. On 18 September 1996 at 11.52 GMT, a Moon–Pluto conjunction will fall within five degrees of the transiting Ascendant. Past experience has shown that whenever this occurs a market fall results and so this day is well worth watching out for. This particular instance of the pattern is unusual and noteworthy because it occurs within trading hours, and will more likely than not cause the market to be distinctly bearish that day. Although two other Moon–Pluto conjunctions also fall quite close to the Ascendant, on 20 December 1995 and 13 February 1996, these both take place outside trading hours and are therefore unlikely to produce such significant effects, although they will tend to depress trading slightly on those days.

In 1997, we expect the market to be quite strong during the first six months, but the second half of the year promises to be very volatile. Large swings of up to 200 points at a time in both directions are likely to take place during this second six-month period.

The summer of 1999 will also be a year when you should watch the market carefully, for on 11 August of that year, a highly ominous-looking planetary configuration takes place. Readers will recall our discussion of the dramatic events produced by the lunar eclipse of August 1990. The effects of the eclipse reverberated powerfully throughout the world, giving rise to significant stock market moves and setting off a disastrous chain of financial consequences for certain individual companies such as Polly Peck. We predict that equally violent results – perhaps even more so – will be produced by the August 1999 eclipse, which this time is a solar one. Indeed, it is not overstating the case to say that this eclipse promises to be one of the worst of the century.

The chart for the eclipse is shown in Fig. 7.1, set for London. Here again, we see a striking picture of a Grand Cross involving the eclipse position. The Sun conjunct Moon in Leo is opposed by Uranus in Aquarius and this pattern is squared by the opposition of Mars in Scorpio to Saturn in Taurus. As in 1990, the middle degrees of the fixed signs – always a significant placement for the markets – are where the action takes place. This potentially violent pattern, drawing in the eclipse, the combination of the explosive Mars–Uranus square and the depressing energies of Saturn, is a certain recipe for trouble in the markets. Further difficulties

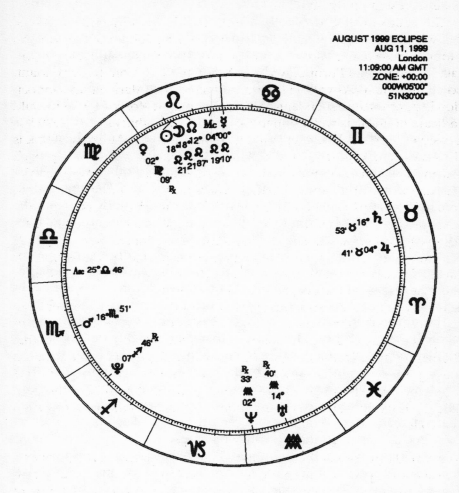

FIGURE 7.1: 11 AUGUST 1999 ECLIPSE

will also be caused by the opposition between Mercury, the planet of trading and communication, and Neptune, the planet of confusion, which is also present on the day.

The eclipse will undoubtedly cause trouble in the world's markets, but which ones will be hardest hit? The eclipse position of the Sun and Moon is close to the Midheaven in London, but makes even closer contact in continental Europe, while in New York it lies on the Ascendant, so all these markets will be severely affected. The Mars–Saturn opposition lies across the Ascendant–Descendant axis in Moscow, which could indicate political as well as financial difficulties in that city. By 1999 it is possible that a stock market could have developed in Moscow: if that is the case, then August 1999 would most certainly be a time to approach that market with extreme caution. Given the violent nature of the eclipse, it is also well worth noting whether, where and how closely it links into individual company charts. To relieve this picture of unrelenting gloom, it should be noted that this eclipse will not automatically spell disaster for every company whose chart it happens to contact! Much depends on the nature of the natal planets that are aspected by the eclipse. If these aspects are positive ones, such as 'eclipse trine Jupiter', for instance, then the effects of the eclipse may be positive too.

Our final and longest-range prediction for the UK stock market is set for 5 June 2007. (Financial astrology enables us to make predictions of the precise day of an event, many years in the future.) We predict that the market will fall at this time, for the Sun will be triggering a Jupiter–Saturn 'falling trine'. Note that 2007 is a key year in the solar four-year cycle when the market is likely to rise strongly in the first months of the year. The top is likely therefore to be 5 June 2007 and a significant correction will follow.

This schedule of predictions reveals the general patterns and major events that we anticipate will unfold over the coming years. Financial astrology is, above all, a highly practical study, which takes the patterns of the past and applies them to the future. Since the bittersweet experience of boom and bust which so vividly typified the *Zeitgeist* of the late 1980s and early 1990s, interest in charting the movements of financial cycles has never been greater. Indeed, those in business who know which way the financial winds are blowing will always be well placed, regardless of whether a storm is brewing or not. So if you wish to understand how the future will unfold, there is no better place to start than with financial astrology – which is, put simply, the study of cycles.

As we have seen, many, many factors are involved in assembling accurate models of financial activity. Even the world's leading financial astrologers freely admit that their knowledge is far from perfect and that they still have much to learn. As a true offspring of the computer age, financial astrology is in a very real sense still in its infancy and if we are to realise its potential fully, still more advanced technology must be brought into play. At the moment, astrologers in the forefront of this field have focused on developing computer programmes to analyse cycles and planetary configurations. But new techniques are still waiting to be developed that will enable all the various stock market indicators to be assessed at one sitting or, indeed, many hundreds or thousands of company charts to be scanned and the handful of businesses where multiple influences are at work at any particular time to be pinpointed.

We hope that our account of financial astrology and what it has to offer has inspired you to incorporate its tools and techniques into your working life. Should you wish to apply the predictive insights of astrology in your own company, then it is essential to work closely with your company chart, for this alone can provide you with the kind of precise, individual forecasts that will ultimately benefit your business most. You can either set up your company chart yourself, using the software listed in the Directory of Resources, or, if you are new to astrology, you may wish to employ the services of a professional astrologer who is skilled in business and financial forecasting. If you decide to take the latter course, you will be joining the ranks of J. P. Morgan and a growing number of successful businessmen the world over who have discovered that using astrology gives them what they most need – a sense of what the future holds. This knowledge alone will give you the vital edge that is indispensable if you wish, as you surely must, to stay ahead in business.

Directory of Resources

Money and the Markets has been written as an introductory text for the general business and investment reader, and as we emphasised at the outset, limitations of space have not allowed us to feature all the tools and techniques that might be of interest to readers seeking to use astrology to improve their business acumen. So, for readers who wish to learn about the more advanced techniques of financial astrology and more about astrology in general, we have compiled a list of books, organisations and computer software that we hope will prove useful.

In addition to the books and articles referenced in the text, the following list provides both introductory and more advanced reading.

Introductory Books

Teach Yourself Astrology, J. Mayo, Hodder Headline, London, 1964.
Although this book has been in print for many years, it is still one of the best beginner's books available. It covers all the basic principles and techniques of astrology in an understandable and thorough way.

Horoscope Symbols, Robert Hand, Para Research, Mass, USA, 1981.
A good second book giving the beginner a deeper understanding of the principles of astrology.

Further Reading

In addition to the books on financial astrology mentioned in the text, the following are suitable for those with a good grasp of basic astrology.

Working with Astrology, M. Harding and C. Harvey, Arkana, London, 1990.
An introduction to more advanced techniques.

Mundane Astrology, M. Baigent, N. Campion and C. Harvey, The Aquarian Press, London, 2nd ed., 1992.
More advanced, but unlike the above books it deals with world affairs rather than personal astrology. One of the best modern introductions to mundane forecasting.

Financial Astrology for the 1990s, Ed. Joan McEvers, Llewellyn, MN, USA, 1989.
A collection of essays dealing with various topics in financial astrology.

Of the books referenced in the text, we would point out particularly those by D. Williams and C. C. Matlock (D. Williams, *Astro-Economics*, Llewellyn, 1959; *Financial Astrology*, American Federation of Astrologers, 1982; C. C. Matlock, *Man and Cosmos*, Development Cycles Research Project, Waynesville, NC, USA, 1977).

Ephemeris Books

The American Ephemeris for the 20th Century, ACS Publications.
A geocentric ephemeris covering the years 1900–2000, giving planetary positions for each day. The publisher also produces smaller volumes, one for each decade.

The American Heliocentric Ephemeris 1901–2000, ACS Publications.

Courses
  The Faculty of Astrological Studies
  396 Caledonian Road
  London N1 1DN

  Tel. 071-700 3556

The main teaching body for astrology, providing an introductory course leading to the Certificate and a more advanced course for the Diploma of the Faculty. The Diploma is a professional level qualification and covers all aspects of modern astrology. The tuition is either by classes in London or by correspondence. The Faculty has students world-wide.

Computer Software
Suppliers of general astrological software include:
  Matrix Software
  PO Box 9
  Pitlochry
  Perthshire
  PH9 0YD

Tel. 0796 473910

A wide range of programs are available, including Blue Star which was used to produce the astrological charts in this book.
  Readers in the USA can contact Matrix at:
  Matrix Software Inc.
  315 Marion Avenue
  Big Rapids, MI 49307
  USA

  Roy Gillett Consultants
  32 Glynswood
  Camberley
  Surrey
  GU15 1HU

  Tel. 0276 683898

Supplies the Astrolabe range of software including the Astro-Analyst program for work in financial astrology. Although it does not cover all the methods used in this book (particularly the double and triple cycle graphs), Astro-Analyst is the most comprehensive financial astrology program available at present.
  Readers in the USA can contact:
  Astrolabe Inc.
  PO Box 1750
  350 Underpass Road
  Brewster, MA 02631
  USA
  Electric Ephemeris
  396 Caledonian Road
  London N1 1DN

  Tel. 071-700 0999

Provides a good, simple program for quickly calculating and displaying charts.

Organisations

The Astrological Association of Great Britain
396 Caledonian Road
London N1 1DN

Tel. 071-700 3746

This is the major astrological organisation in the UK and also has a large international membership. It is open to all levels from beginner to professional. It publishes a journal six times a year containing articles on all aspects of astrology. In addition it holds an annual conference and week-end seminars, including its Mundane Astrology Day and Research Conference. The research journal *Correlation* is published twice a year and is an important source for current research work.

The Urania Trust
396 Caledonian Road
London N1 1DN

Tel. 071-700 0639

The co-ordination body for UK astrology and the main source of information. An annual guide to events in the UK and Europe containing the addresses of the main astrological bodies in each country is available by sending a large stamped addressed envelope or two International Reply Coupons if writing from outside the UK.

NCGR
105 Snyder Ave
Ramsey, NJ 07446
USA

The leading US astrological organisation, it publishes a journal dealing with all aspects of astrology.

Foundation for the Study of Cycles Inc.
900 West Valley Road
Suite 502
Wayne
PA 19087
USA

Tel 0101 215 995 2120

As pointed out in Chapter 2, the Foundation is the major organisation engaged in cycles research. It publishes *Cycles*, a magazine covering all aspects of research, including economic, stock and commodity market cycles and cycles in nature. Its catalogue lists many books and articles dealing with cycles, and a number of otherwise hard to obtain books.

Index